WHAT HEALTH CARE PROFESSIONALS SAY ABOUT *BABYWISE*

In the morass of recently published books on parenting, this exceedingly practical manual emerges as a beacon of guidance, wisdom, and common sense. Parents of all backgrounds will benefit from the time-tested methods presented. I have interacted with children raised in this method first-hand and can attest to scores of well-adjusted children who are a joy to their parents. I wholeheartedly endorse this manual without reservation.

Jonathan L. Scott, M.D., Ph.D.
Los Angeles, CA

Medical school in no way prepared me for one of the more demanding aspects of my practice, dealing with infant feeding. The theory of feeding a baby whenever it cries, which was standard teaching, was not only without justification, it simply did not meet the needs of my patients. Since being introduced to the principles of *BABYWISE*, I have been convinced of its effectiveness in establishing sleep patterns and in decreasing the frequency of problems associated with infant feeding. If thriving children and happy, rested parents were not enough, my greatest commendation of *BABYWISE* is that my own children are being raised by these precepts.

Craig Lloyd, M.D.
Brisbane, Australia

As a pediatrician, I cannot argue with the success of *BABYWISE*. It is such a practical approach to parenting. It provides infants with needed structure and stability and brings the joy and love so needed in our homes today. The effects of not using *BABYWISE* show up very quickly. That is why I have made these principles a priority of discussion in every well-child care visit. Parents constantly tell me, "It changed our lives."

Janet Dahmen, M.D.
Chatsworth, CA

As family physicians and a husband-wife team, we are often asked questions related to parenting and the general care of children. Most of our basic responses are found in *BABYWISE*. For answering parenting questions, it has become a practical guide giving us a sense of competence and confidence as physicians and as parents. When the principles are put into practice, parents reap abundant rewards.

Tony and Margaret Burden, M.D.
Bellingham, WA

As an obstetrician and a mother, my concern for a healthy outcome continues beyond the moment of delivery. Because the principles of *BABYWISE* are so effective, I consider it part of my extended health care for the entire family. The principles are simple—yet amazing. They consistently produce babies who are healthy, content, and who sleep through the night at an early age. Feeding a baby on demand simply cannot compare to the overall healthy benefits of *BABYWISE*. The concepts take the guesswork out of early parenting and provide new moms the confidence of knowing what happens next. Not following the principles of *BABYWISE* is a potential health concern.

Sharon Nelson, M.D.
Glendale, CA

As a clinical associate professor of obstetrics and gynecology, a certified nurse-midwife, childbirth educator, and a mom, I would be doing a disservice to my patients if I did not direct them to *BABYWISE*. The infant management theories of the last twenty-five years have been rendered useless in light of the tremendous success of this program. Why would any parent not want a happy, healthy, and content baby who sleeps through the night in the first two months? Why would any parent not desire the confidence *BABYWISE* offers? *BABYWISE* wisdom, common sense, confidence—all refreshing and hopeful words for expectant parents to feast upon.

Diane Dirks, C.N.M.,
Pasadena, CA

As a mother, I have parented both ways. As a certified lactation educator, I only recommend *BABYWISE*. I know how discouraging it is to feed a baby around the clock with no apparent advantage. I know how tired a young mom can get and how that affects her milk supply. I also know how discouraging the first eighteen months of parenting can be without a plan. I know because with my first child I did everything the opposite of *BABYWISE*. Before my second baby was born, I was introduced to the concepts presented in this book. Applying the principles revolutionized my thinking. Instead of being in baby bondage, I was liberated to be the mother God wanted me to be. I have consistently used *BABYWISE* with the women I counsel. These mothers have met with tremendous success, whether bottle or breast-feeding. *BABYWISE* is proactive, preventative parenting, minimizing the common problems often associated with breast-feeding.

Barbara Phillips, R.N., C.L.E.
Los Angeles, CA

As a practicing pediatrician, husband, and father, I enthusiastically recommend *BABYWISE*. I found the principles contained within to be a sigh of welcome relief to sleepless, weary parents and more than an ounce of prevention for those who adopt these concepts from the start. I am convinced that the well-tested principles of *BABYWISE* produce confident parents, secure and content infants, and peaceful and orderly homes.

David Blank, M.D.
Longmont, CO

I am a practicing pediatrician and assistant professor of pediatrics. Residents and new mothers I work with have found *BABYWISE* over-whelmingly successful. My residents report a positive difference in the confidence of new mothers who work with this plan compared to those who do not. The freedom *BABYWISE* provides a new mother is so refreshing. Life is predictable, allowing her to be proactive in parenting, not reactive, which usually produces less than desirable results. My parents become baby wise with *BABYWISE*.

Linda Meloy, M.D.
Richmond, VA

On Becoming

BABYWISE

Gary Ezzo & Robert Bucknam, M.D.

GROWING FAMILIES
INTERNATIONAL

On Becoming BABYWISE

Published by Growing Families International Press,
9259 Eton Avenue
Chatsworth, California 91311

Printed in the United States of America
Library of Congress Catalog Card Number: TX 562 499

ISBN:1-883035-99-6

Dedicated to:

Dr. Fred and Mary Barshaw
For their many years
of lighting the way.

CONTENTS

FOREWARD

After completing medical school and serving my residency in obstetrics and gynecology, I felt knowledgeable enough to be a parent. Between my wife's degree in child development and my medical training, how hard could this parenting thing be? We would just do what comes naturally and follow our instincts. Right? Wrong!

Soon after the birth of our first son, we quickly found our enthusiasm and confidence turned into exhaustion and frustration. Mom was up three times at night and the baby was cranky during the day. The unsolicited advice typically offered was to feed the baby more often since he was obviously hungry. We did feed him, around the clock, every two hours. So much for instincts.

Scientists can put a man on the moon, but they cannot answer the most basic problems of early parenting: how to have a happy and contented baby who sleeps continually through the night like the rest of the family and a mother who is not in a perpetual state of exhaustion.

Through our common interest in children and parenting, my wife and I became acquainted with the work and accomplishments of Gary and Anne Marie Ezzo of *Growing Families International*. The Ezzo's basic and loving concepts for nurturing newborns virtually eliminated the problems listed above and many more. I have personally observed both infants who were guided by the Ezzo's principles and those who were not. It became obvious that parents equipped with the right information do make a difference.

I have since made the transition from obstetrics to pediatrics and with the switch came the medically sound principles of *BABYWISE*. They work consistently, not only for the thousands of children already touched by *Growing Families International*, but also for my three children, my colleagues' children, my friends' children, and now, for all my patients.

To say the least, *BABYWISE* has brought a needed reformation to pediatric counsel given to new parents. When parents come in looking exhausted and discouraged and tell me their woeful stories of sleepless nights and fussy babies, I can give them a positive prescription that cures the problem—I hand them *BABYWISE*.

Robert Bucknam, M.D.
Louisville, Colorado

PREFACE

Yes, one day people will stop you on the street, at the grocery store, and in the church nursery to comment, "Your baby is so content." Then they will insult you with the following commentary: "You're so lucky to have such an easy baby. What? Sleeping through the night already? How old is he? You're *really* lucky!"

As philosopher Immanuel Kant pointed out, the actual proves the possible. With *BABYWISE*, we no longer count the success stories in thousands, but in tens of thousands. *BABYWISE* is not a book of luck but of principle. Luck has nothing to do with the benefits described above—right parenting does. What you do in the first days, weeks, and months of your baby's life will impact the rest of your parenting years.

This is more than a sleep-training book. Getting your baby to sleep through the night within six to eight weeks is the easiest part of parenting. Realizing the awesome duty of raising a responsible human being is more difficult.

This book will not provide you with a list of rules. We

wish parenting were that easy. Our purpose is to get you started on the right track, beginning with the preparation of your mind, which is far more important than the preparation of the nursery. Your baby will not care if his head rests on designer sheets or on Disney characters. His behavior will not be ordered by his wardrobe or by his bedroom accessories, but by the mindset that dictates how you live your life.

Our personal perspective of life in general governs how we relate to our children, to our spouse, and to others. This book assumes that the reader is family-centered and is not child-centered. That means you regard your baby as a welcome member of the family and not the center of the family universe. That perspective is foundational to the concepts presented in this book.

In discussing infant and maternal physiology, we will demonstrate how order and stability are mutual allies of every newborn's metabolism. In particular, we will note how an infant's body responds to the influences of parental routine, or the lack thereof.

In the latter chapters, we will explore the everyday aspects of infant management. Included is an explanation of the three basic elements of daytime activities for newborns: feeding time, waketime, and naptime.

The questions at the end of each chapter emphasize the key themes found in your reading. We encourage you to take the time to go through and write out the answers. You will feel more confident when you know *what* to do and *why* you should do it. We designed the study questions to serve as an aid in gaining that confidence.

BABYWISE is more than an infant-management concept; it is a mindset for responsible parenthood. The principles presented will help any parent develop a plan that meets both the needs of a new baby and of the entire family. This plan will not leave Mom ragged at the end of the day nor in bondage to her child. Nor will Dad be excluded from his duties. These principles have worked for thousands of parents and, when faithfully applied, will also work wonderfully for you!

Gary Ezzo

INTRODUCTION

We would like to introduce two fictional characters who will appear at various times throughout this book. Their names are Ryan and Nathan—cousins born within a week of each other. Ryan's parents followed the principles presented in this book; Nathan's parents did not. Although these are fictional characters, the differences stated in their development are factual.

To remain consistent with these characters, we have chosen to use the masculine gender *he* throughout this book. The principles, of course, work equally well with both genders.

1

YOUR BABY NEEDS A FAMILY

Because the family is the primary social unit of every society, it is also the most important—one worth protecting and keeping. As professionals providing health and educational services to children and parents, we know the tragedy that can befall a family when basic principles of parenting are violated. We have counseled parents who started with the best intentions to love and nurture, only to see their dreams of a beautiful family reduced to a nightmare of survival. The problem was not wrong motives but wrong methods.

There are two related evils that threaten successful parenting. The first is not rightly understanding the significance of the husband-wife relationship in the parenting process, and the second is the danger of child-centered parenting.

THE GREATEST INFLUENCE

The greatest overall influence you will have on your children will not come in your role as an individual, but in your joint role as husband and wife. That basic truth has been forgotten, resulting in a society consumed with child centeredness, self-centeredness, and self-fulfillment. The emotional and physical detriment to children is the ultimate consequence.

As professionals, we cannot overstate how necessary a healthy husband-wife relationship is to the emotional well being of children. Many times parents lose sight of the fact that when their children enter the family, they enter an established social structure. Parents often act as if the marriage union were only a preliminary relationship to child rearing rather than perceiving it as an ongoing priority relationship.

Maintaining the marriage relationship as a priority is necessary for successful parenting. The quality of the parent-child relationship depends upon the quality of the husband-wife relationship. Of all Ryan's emotional needs, his most basic one is knowing that his world is secure. What he observes between his mom and dad establishes that sense of security. As he observes their emotional togetherness in the normal course of a day, he is more secure simply because he does not have to question the legitimacy of their commitment to one another.

All children are born with a radar device that hones in on parental conflict. If a child perceives more weakness than strength, it produces a low-level anxiety that ultimately affects his ability to learn. A child knows intuitively, just as his parents knew when they were growing up, that if something happens to his mom and dad, his whole world will collapse. If the parents' relationship is always in question in the mind of a child, then the child will live his life on the brink of disaster.

Ryan's mom can spend 24 hours a day loving and nurturing him, but all that sacrificial time and attention can never meet Ryan's need to know that his mom loves his dad. His dad can buy all sorts of toys and play with him for hours, but that will not satisfy the greatest desire of Ryan's heart: to know his dad and mom love each other.

When a child has confidence in his parents' relationship, he is emotionally free to get on with life. When there is harmony in the husband-wife relationship, there is an infused stability within the family. Strong marriages provide a haven of security for children as they grow.

CHILD-CENTERED PARENTING

Often, in the name of good parenting, moms and dads leave their first love—each other—and focus totally on their children. That refocusing is the first step to the breakup of the family, leading to the second threat to successful parenting: the belief that children are to be the center of the family universe.

Nathan's parents believe that falsity. As a result, they are willing to gamble the future of the whole family. They base their practice on the belief that good parenting is determined solely by the amount of attention and sacrifice given to children. Nathan will never have to wait for anything. If he cries, his parents will pick him up immediately. If he wants something, he will get it. No babysitters for Nathan. If he can't go with his parents, they don't go. If he doesn't like his baby food, no problem; his Mom will offer a variety of choices until she finds something he likes.

Nathan's parents do not realize that all their good intentions are fostering an emotional disability we call *me-ism*. Nathan's perception of his place in life depends significantly on the feedback and stimulation he receives from the people outside of himself. If that stimulation is such that it leads him to perceive himself to be the center of the family, he will develop a self-centered perception that will carry into every relationship he forms as his world expands.

We have seen the devastating results of that style of parenting. Nathan's potential for failure in basic relationships will increase because other people simply will not matter to him. He will have difficulty getting along with siblings and peers. He will grow up ill-prepared for real life, where the ability to give and take is a prerequisite for healthy and enduring relationships. Because other significant people will not cater to him as quickly as his mom and dad do, life for Nathan will become terribly frustrating.

In contrast, Ryan's mom and dad are raising him with an eye toward integrating his life into the already-existing family structure. They are creating within their son a propensity for close and loving relationships. When a child perceives himself as a welcome member of the family, he gradually learns to integrate into other social relationships with both flexibility and confidence. For any child, being a welcome member of the family produces a *we-ism* attitude. That attitude accepts one's role in the family as a team member—where giving is as important as receiving.

FRIENDSHIP AND CONFORMITY

Ryan's parents believe they are obligated to produce a responsible human being and are not willing to leave that goal to chance. They accept the challenge of parenting, realizing the process of training starts with them. For Ryan, belonging to his family is not an option, but a mandate. His parents expect certain behavior out of him and are willing to force conformity when required. They believe there are certain virtues worth acquiring, such as kindness, goodness, gentleness, charity, honesty, honor, and respect.

Since these qualities are not naturally found in Ryan's tiny little life, they must be nurtured into his heart. Ryan's parents accept their role as loving governors. That is, they will govern his life until they have developed within his heart the self-control and the moral precepts that will allow him to govern himself. That freedom comes gradually—from the playpen to the backyard, and then to the neighborhood. As Ryan demonstrates responsible behavior and sound judgment, he earns another level of freedom. That type of training results in a child who is a joy to everyone and has achieved a sense of affirmation within himself.

In contrast, Nathan's mom and dad are following a different philosophy of parenting. They believe that good parenting only requires them to be friends with their child, and thus they treat him as a peer. Unfortunately, no one informed them of the consequences of such thinking. With that style of parenting, family relationships for Nathan will always be optional.

This theory of child rearing, called *democratic parenting*,[1] is based on making everyone equal in the family, in hopes of eliminating all naughty behavior from the life of the child.[2] Nathan's mom and dad act more like his buddies than his parents, even abandoning the two terms of endearment that are so special in the life of every little boy and girl, "*Daddy*" and "*Mommy*." Instead, using their first names is acceptable: Nathan can just call them Bob and Sue.

Who would not want to be friends with their children? From a parenting perspective, what can sound more noble or captivating than a family made up of friends? Certainly that is an admirable idea, especially appealing to a generation who may have wondered about the lack of friendship with their own parents. But is it right?

When parents remove terms of endearment (and the relationships they represent) from a child's life, they sever a major strand that ties together close relationships. Maybe that severance is one reason democratic parenting has failed over the last twenty years. That fact may also explain why our society saw the proliferation of teenage rebellion and broken families in the 1970s and 1980s.

Being your child's friend is not the starting point of your parenting, but the relational goal. Friendship is what you are attempting to achieve by the end of the teen years. Of course, you will still have fun with your children. You can still be buddies during the training process. Successful parenting requires that a parent not devalue his or her role, reducing it to the level of the child. Neither should a parent elevate the child to the level of a peer.

Time and experience are prerequisites for building any friendship. Children are not born with the benefit of having wisdom, experience, or self-control. Once you entered parenthood, you became responsible for training your child. Nature automatically grants you the right to make decisions in your child's best interest.

Responsible parenthood means that you are the teacher and they are the students. You lead; they follow. There will be plenty of time for friendship later and with responsible parenting plenty of reason for it. Right training will always lead to the conclusion of true friendship. By proxy, Ryan's parents represent his best interests. As his mother and father, they know what is best for him and will insist on compliance—even conformity. For Ryan, family relationships have meaning and purpose. He belongs to something bigger than himself—he belongs to his family.

ACHIEVING A BALANCE

Becoming child-centered is easy when you have a baby. Infants are totally dependent on parental care, and that heightens the gratification of the parenting experience. However, there are ways that you can meet all your baby's needs and not be child-centered. Here are a few ideas that can help you achieve that balance.

1. Remind yourself that life does not stop once you have a baby. It may slow down for a few weeks, but it does not stop completely. When you become a mother, you do not stop being a daughter, a sister, a friend, or a wife. Those relationships were important to you before the baby. Be sure to maintain them afterwards.

2. If you had a weekly date night with your spouse before the baby was born, continue that practice as soon as you can, letting friends or relatives watch the baby. A child does not go through separation anxiety when his mom is with his dad. If you did not have a weekly date night, start now. Your date does not have to be an expensive or late evening.

3. Do not stop doing those special gestures for each other that you once did before children came into your lives. If there was a special activity you both enjoyed previously, plan it into your schedule. If a husband brings home a gift for the baby, he should also bring flowers for his wife. The idea here is basic—continue to do those loving gestures that marked your relationship as special and keep it special.

4. Invite friends over for a meal or for an evening of fellowship. By focusing on these times of hospitality, you are forced to focus on your house. That distraction is healthy, because it obligates you to plan your child's day around serving other people.

5. Practice *couch time*. When the workday is over, take fifteen minutes and sit on the couch together as a couple. That event should take place when the chil-

dren are awake, not after they have gone to bed. You can explain to them, "No unnecessary interruptions are allowed because this is Mommy and Daddy's special time together. Daddy will play with Ryan afterwards, but Mommy comes first." Couch time provides a visual sense of your togetherness. In this tangible way a child can measure his mommy and daddy's love relationship and have that inner need satisfied. In addition, couch time provides a predictable forum for a couple to share their relational needs with each other.

SUMMARY

We desire that your family life be filled with joy, abound in sweet memories, and untainted by regret. That is not a statement of idealism but one of direction and encouragement. Priority relationships are not arbitrary. They are not dictated by circumstances or by social fads. Relationships within the family function best when parents orchestrate them to the common goal of love and family unity.

If you desire to achieve excellence in parenting, you must protect your marriage. A strong marriage acts as the stabilizing factor against the shocks of life. As you maintain that priority relationship, you are simultaneously hedging against child-centered parenting. The relationship you have with your child should be that of parent, teacher, and governor. He is not your peer, but someone who needs your guiding hand. From the beginning, he is a welcome member of the family but never the center of it.

Finally, work toward the goal of your child's friendship, remembering it is not the starting point of your relationship, but the objective.

QUESTIONS FOR REVIEW

1. Of all Ryan's basic emotional needs, which is the most basic?

2. What happens when a child perceives weakness in his parents' relationship?

3. What is the first step to breaking up a family?

4. What emotional disability does child-centered parenting produce?

5. How long should parents act as governors in the lives of their children?

6. The theory of democratic parenting is based on what two assumptions?

7. What is the role of friendship in the parenting process?

2

FEEDING PHILOSOPHIES

One would assume that establishing good feeding habits would be the easiest feature of child training, since the drive to obtain nourishment is one of the strongest in all living creatures. But much more occurs during your baby's feeding time than just filling up a little tummy. Your choice in parenting philosophy will actually determine your child's hunger patterns, sleep patterns, and even his basic disposition.

DEFINING THE TERMS
New and expectant parents can easily become confused over the terminology associated with today's ever expanding feeding philosophies. During your pregnancy, you may have been encouraged to "demand-feed" your new arrival, while at the same time warned not to follow a "schedule," especially if you intended to breast-feed. Maybe you have heard about a "demand-schedule" or a "self-demand schedule." Perhaps you have been told to consider "natural feeding" for your baby. Avoid "hyperscheduling," some would say, because that is "rigid-feeding," and rigid-

feeding is not as good as "cry-feeding." Yet, cry-feeding is supposedly less desirable than "cue-feeding," which is similar to "responsive-feeding." And what about "bottle-feeding"? Is this a new twentieth-century concept practiced only by the modern mother?

Where did those terms come from and what do they mean? By reviewing social and historical feeding practices, we can gain insight into the philosophy, methodology, and even the mythology associated with infant feeding.

Prior to this century, common sense was the rule for raising children, not theoretical concepts. Mothers nursed their babies when they were hungry, but with guidance. The mother guided the hunger cycles of the baby to match her routine for the welfare of the entire family. Mothers of the past were not clock watchers; they did not have to be. They had a natural schedule set by their domestic duties. Routine and predictable feeding periods fit into a schedule that met the needs of their babies and the entire family. It was that simple.

As the industrial revolution progressed, new infant management theories evolved. During this century, two theories have dominated American parenting. The first was introduced in the early years by a group of scientists called "behaviorists," who acted on the assumption that a child would become what his environment dictated. They placed a greater emphasis on outward structure than on developing emotions and feelings. The belief among behaviorists was that controlled environments produced controlled emotions.

In the early 1920s, the American mother was introduced to a form of infant feeding called *hyperscheduling* or *clock-feeding*. Established was a strict 4-hour feeding schedule, and mothers followed it to the minute. If a baby appeared hungry after 3 hours, too bad, he would just have to wait until the fourth hour. The clock was the final authority on feeding times regardless of the needs of the baby or his mom.[3]

By the mid-1940s, an adaptation of Sigmund Freud's child-rearing theories started to nudge out the rigidness of behaviorism. Freud's twentieth-century followers stressed the instinctual, animal-like qualities of infancy as the starting point for child management.

Structure was not as important to those theorists as were the child's developing emotions. With revisions made to Freud's theories, the American parent was pulled to the other extreme. Now when the baby cried, he was to be fed immediately, whether he was hungry or not. It was postulated that nursing would satisfy nutritional and presumed psychological needs.

To what type of psychological need were these theorists referring? Psychoanalysts attempted to locate the origin and nature of adult neuroses by isolating significant traumatic experiences in early childhood. Originally the quest into the past terminated in the preschool years (two or three years of age). When no traumatic experiences were discovered in the average patient, analysts were forced to either abandon their theory or, by faith, move to the conclusion that the original source of traumatic experience was the birthing process itself (Otto Rank, 1929). Even Freud greeted such a notion in his day with considerable skepticism.

It was hypothesized that lodged in a child's subconscious memory is the trauma of birth, which separated the child from the pleasurable primal state of the mother. As a result of the birth shock, the child has an unconscious yearning to return to the safety and security of the womb. Since it is presumed that the baby remains psychologically fragile for the first two or three years of life, the mother's job is to create a constant womb like environment that will protect him.

That belief inspired the neoprimitivistic school of child care, supported by Ribble (1944); Aldrich (1945); Trainham, Pilafian, and Kraft (1945); and Frank (1945). The title "neoprimitivistic" is not name-calling, but a specific school of thought. This theory postulates that the separation at birth momentarily interrupts the mother-child *in utero* harmony. Therefore, the goal of early parenting is to reestablish that harmony. How is this supposed to be achieved? Only by the constant day-and-night presence and availability of the mother to the child. New mothers are instructed to do whatever it takes to neutralize the supposed trauma of birth and offset its effect.

The birth-trauma theory suffered from the lack of objective verifiable data and was dismissed by 1949, only to resurface twenty-five years later repackaged with some slight modifications under the title *attachment parenting*. In truth it is not attachment parenting but reattachment parenting. What is proposed in the modern version is remarkably similar to the 1940s version, when mothers were told to endlessly carry their babies, sleep with them, breast-feed them day and night without regard to any routine, and breast-feed them well into their second or third year. Toilet training was to take place very late, perhaps not until the child decided voluntarily to become potty trained. Parents exalted the child as the center of the family universe and designed their parenting practices so as to avoid conflict, anxiety, and discomfort so that he would not grow up with a debilitating psychosis. (Actually, if you parent that way, you yourself may end up with some form of psychosis.) Today, there are no limits as to how far a mother can go to create what she considers to be an anxiety-free environment.

As a result of that speculation, the American mother in the early 1950s was nudged to a nonstructured approach to parenting. First, Dr. Benjamin Spock rightly rejected the behaviorist's assumptions of absolute structure and moved his patients toward structure mixed with flexibility. Authorizing mothers to use flexibility in their schedule was a radical concept in the 1950s—and a needed course correction. By 1970, Spock's views were pushed out by the practice of feeding on demand. The baby's cry replaced the clock and a parent-guided flexible routine.

There are two basic assumptions inherent with the term *feeding on demand*. First, parents assume that "baby knows best" and reject any type of parent-guided routine. Second, the signal for food is the baby's cry, and parents assume every cry is a request for food (or, as borrowed from the birth trauma theory, for psychological comfort).

We are strongly critical of such rigid advice. Some newborns may not cry to signal hunger readiness for 5-6 hours, and crying is not always a signal of hunger. Weak and sickly babies may not have the energy to cry, thus allowing serious medical problems to go unnoticed.

NOTE: From this point forward, when we refer to the practice of demand-feeding, we are implying the following: The cry of a baby is the primary signal for nursing, whether it be for food or a presumed psychological need regardless of how much time has elapsed since the last nursing period. The philosophy of demand-feeding rejects any thought of a parent-guided routine.

By the early 1980s, the neoprimitivistic school of infant care and its attachment theories gained more ground. Attachment theorists subscribe to the doctrine of "felt needs" as the cue for care and training. Demand-feeding and immediate gratification are primary parts of the attachment process. These theories suggest that the sensitivity that helps a mother do the right thing at the right time develops more quickly (and to a greater degree) through nursing. That is why you supposedly can never nurse too long or too often. All wants are to be interpreted as needs—even for a three year old. When a three year old signals for a snack by pulling on his mother's blouse, and his mother offers him the breast, even if only for a minute, she is acting on the belief that he still has an attachment need. According to the theory, to say no is to deny him love when he needs it.[4]

Possibly the child does have a need. But is it the result of birth trauma or a philosophy of parenting? Might the methods used to manufacture a secure attachment child be an essential part of the problem? Could the results be so obvious that we ignore them? The kind of close inter-action and involvement associated with demand-style par-enting works against a child's good development. These theorists give no thought to the possibility that they are actually training mothers to misinterpret their baby's cues. As a result, the parenting style and not the throw of the genetic dice is responsible for producing the symptoms of the emotionally stressed "high-need" baby. Those symp-toms, (in contrast to the results of BABYWISE), include the combination of excessive fussiness and colic-like symp-toms, disequilibrium in feeding and sleep cycles, waking throughout the night for up to two years, perpetual need for comfort nursing, fear of mother separation, fear of sleeping by himself, desire for immediate gratification, lack of self-comforting coping skills, limited self-play adeptness, a demanding pretoddler and toddler, and one tired mom. To add insult to injury, they blame the mother not the theory, when everything falls apart—sometimes including the marriage. Our point is this: in hopes of meeting every need of the psychologically fragile child, one is actually created.

The weakness of the birth trauma theory, from birth to weaning, is found in its premise. Does the birthing process create psychologically fragile children? It is doubtful whether newborns experience anxiety as a result of birth or have any memory of it. Neither conscious or unconscious memory function can take place in the low-oxygen environment of the uterus. Memory function and synapse development depend on the brain receiving highly oxygenated blood, which comes from breathing. Breathing cannot begin until the lungs inflate, and that occurs after birth. In addition, higher brain centers are still developing at the time of birth.

For the sake of argument, let us assume there is the possibility of a functioning memory in the prebirth state. If we were to attribute wishes, hopes, and fears to the unborn, we would have to assume that toward the end of the pregnancy, the child longs to be born, since his environment is no longer a paradise. The squirming, turning, wrenching, jerking, and kicking in the last month forces the assumption that the child is more eager to be freed from his present environment than desirous of staying in it. The womb restrains and holds him back from liberation.

What about the memories of restraint created in the last month? Do they produce a reservoir of anxiety? Could womb confinement be the original source of trauma? Is any of the above possible? Once you open the door of speculation regarding memory function in a prebirth state, all sorts of logical (yet bizarre) theories are possible.

Although variations of neoprimitivistic and attachment parenting theories have a fad-like character, they are not well-grounded on an impeccable body of empirical data. There is plenty of hopeful speculation, but only a minimum amount of objective and verifiable information. To date, no one has demonstrated a relationship between the birthing experience and later neurosis (or the birthing experience and any neurosis).

While behaviorists emphasize outward structure and not the inner person, the neoprimitivistic school emphasizes the inner person at the expense of outward structure. As professionals, we believe both approaches are extreme, wrong, and detrimental to the healthy development of a baby and soon-to-be toddler. We offer an alternative to parents. You can have structure and still meet all the developing needs of your baby with PDF.

SUMMARY

Some mothers emotionally thrive on an attachment style of parenting. For them, womanhood means motherhood. That is not the case for all women and for this latter group there is an alternative—*parent-directed feeding* (PDF). Our premises are basic. We believe that when a woman becomes a mother, she does not stop being a wife, daughter, sister, friend, or neighbor. Regarding feeding and a newborn, our conviction is that a baby should be fed when he signals readiness. With PDF, a mother feeds her baby when he is hungry, but she takes advantage of the first few weeks to guide his hunger patterns by a basic routine. This is cooperative parenting. Because routine feedings wonderfully influence the hunger metabolism of an infant, she guides feeding times for her baby to meet his needs as well as those of the entire family. Both parent and child cooperate in the effort. Because the child is a welcome member and not the center of the family, and because he is not as emotionally fragile as attachment theorist believe, everyone wins— baby, mother, father, and the often-forgotten siblings.

QUESTIONS FOR REVIEW

1. During this century, what were the two predominant views of infant management? What did they emphasize?

2. What is the birth-trauma theory? What does it require from a mother?

3. What are two basic assumptions inherent in the title *feeding on demand*?

   a.

   b.

4. List some symptoms of the emotionally-stressed *high-need* baby.

5. List the two basic premises of *parent-directed feeding.*

   a.

   b.

3

THE BENEFITS OF ORDER

Anyone seeking to understand the value of an infant routine must first free his or her mind from two popular misconceptions. One is the assumption that an infant routine detracts from meeting a baby's physical and emotional needs and that somehow the word *schedule* is not compatible with the words *love, caring,* and *concern.* The second misconception is that an infant fed on demand will be happier, healthier, and generally more secure than the one fed by routine because his parents continuously and immediately respond to his cry without assessment. In both cases, nothing could be further from the truth.

Parent-Directed Feeding

As parents, you will want to pursue a course that is best for your baby. That course includes paying attention to your baby's need for outward structure and attention to his developing emotions. The principles of *BABYWISE,* and particularly in the parent-directed feeding guidelines, strike the right balance between the two.

PDF is a proactive approach to infant care. It creates and maintains for your baby a stable outward structure that enhances metabolic and neurologic stabilization. At the same time, PDF is flexible enough to meet the growing emotional needs of the child. That flexibility is a major distinction from the extremes of psychoanalytical thought and behaviorism.

The Need for Order

Order speaks of routine and scheduling. Unfortunately, there are still some whose only understanding of an infant schedule comes from old wives' tales and bad advice. They speak of rigid feeding periods when a baby cries needlessly, waiting to be fed, while his mother hardens her heart to her baby's cry. Although that description may be an accurate reflection of parenting in the 1920s, it is not what an infant schedule should be, nor what parent-directed feeding is all about.

The PDF plan involves more than just feeding a baby. It is a 24-hour strategy designed to meet not only the baby's needs, but those of the entire family. PDF is made up of three basic activities that are repeated in a rhythmical cycle throughout the day: feeding time, waketime, and naptime. Those cycles are both *routine* and *predictable.*

Before we progress further, we need to note the difference between the terms routine and predictable. That which is routine is predictable, but that which may be predictable is not always routine. For example, Ryan's mom follows the principles of PDF. As a result, her interaction with him is both predictable and routine. That is, approximately the same amount of time passes from one feeding event to the next. As we will discuss later, this is an important first step in establishing continuous nighttime sleep.

Nathan's mom is following a demand-feeding approach. As a result, her interaction is very predictable (Nathan cries and she responds), but it is not routine. One hour may pass between two feedings. He cries; she feeds him again. Then, 3 hours may pass the next time, followed by 2 hours. Although feeding for Nathan is predictable, it is also very erratic. The erratic nature of the free-feed theory negatively impacts Nathan's metabolism.

In contrast, Ryan's mom understands the benefits of routine, and she appreciates the accompanying sense of security. Her baby shows by his positive response to routine that he has an inner need for an outward system of structure. Although *in utero* nutrition continually passes on to the baby, there are spikes of nutritional consumption. Those times correlate with the mother's basic three-meals-a-day routine. Outside the womb, a basic feeding routine provides structure that encourages the natural rhythms of a child to synchronize with those of the rest of the family.

For example, infants are not born with a mature central nervous system. Regular and predictable parental interaction is needed to balance a baby's body functions until the central nervous system is mature enough to take over. In contrast, the lack of regularity sends a negative signal to the baby's body, creating metabolic confusion that negatively affects his hunger, digestive, and sleep/wake cycles.

The importance of an infant schedule is well recognized. In most neonatal units, you will find that premature infants, twins, triplets, and low-birthweight babies are not allowed to feed on demand but are placed on a strict three-hour feeding schedule. The reason? Medical authorities know that when you deal with life-and-death situations, babies thrive better when fed on routine as compared to nonroutine feedings. The PDF principles reflect such conservative care.

Putting Ryan on a flexible schedule benefits not only him, but his mom as well. She now has the confidence of knowing what happens next. Life becomes more predictable for her, for Ryan, and for the rest of the family. She can plan her day's activities, knowing that Ryan's needs will be met. That results in a proactive style of parenting rather than a reactive one, which is usually less than satisfactory.

Ryan's mom is also healthier as a result of feeding her baby on a routine. She has the time to get restful sleep and the exercise she needs. As a breast-feeding mom, she is more likely to be successful with a daily infant plan than with random feeding periods. If Ryan has siblings, a plan will allow his mom and dad to give them needed time as well. Everyone wins with PDF.

In contrast, Nathan's mom is so concerned about his developing emotions that she has depreciated the importance of structure. Physical structure is what helps balance his emotions. To compensate, Nathan's parents are more susceptible to every new fad or gadget coming out on the parenting market that promises to settle him down—everything from an electric crib rocker to a teddy bear with a mother-sounding heart beat, and even to nightly drives in the car—all to get him to sleep. There is a better way.

One cannot help but feel sorry for Nathan's parents. They have been victimized by wrong philosophies and, as a result, everyone in the family suffers. Without common sense in a parent's thinking, the most obvious solutions to basic sleep problems are no longer options.

THE ADVANTAGES OF THE PDF

The parent-directed feeding plan has many advantages. It

benefits Ryan, his mom, and his dad in a number of different ways. Here is a partial list of the benefits of this plan.

For Ryan

1. Ryan's metabolism is stabilized, since parental interaction is regular and predictable.

2. Ryan's digestive system will have fewer problems with gastric reflux or with colic-like symptoms when compared with his cry-fed cousin.

3. Ryan's nighttime sleep cycles will be stabilized. Between the third and eighth week, his mom can expect him to sleep 7-8 hours through the night. Ryan will probably sleep 10-12 hours per night by week twelve. By that time, his cousin Nathan will still be waking twice in the middle of the night for a snack and is apt to continue in that pattern for the next two years.

4. Ryan does not have to be manipulated to sleep. When bedtime comes, Ryan's mom and dad place him in his crib, and he falls asleep. If there is any fussing, it is usually very limited. In contrast, Nathan's mother tries to nurse him to sleep, but the ordeal sometimes takes hours. As soon as she puts him in his crib, he is likely to wake up, and she is forced to start the process all over. That style of parenting grows old very quickly.

5. Ryan's stimulus barrier matures more quickly. Nathan, Ryan's cousin, tends to experience unsettledness and startles more easily during the day and night.

6. PDF facilitates the natural process of infants moving

from dependence to independence. The nature of the program fosters *relational* security. That is, a baby's security depends on his developing relationships, not on his proximity to his mother. In contrast, mothers who are constantly attentive by way of baby slings, shared sleep, and demand feeding, all in hopes of fostering security, too often accomplish the opposite. That statement is easily proven. Just remove the child from Mom at any point and observe how secure he appears. It is disheartening to a parent to see his child in a state of hysteria under the stress of independence, while other children the same age are maturing in their independence.

7. Ryan is more accepting of other care-givers from his earliest days, since he receives comfort from other care-givers.

8. PDF fosters an environment of learning from the beginning. Ryan is learning to be at peace with his environment, therefore enhancing his learning potential. Learning disorders associated with nonstructured styles of parenting, including deficiencies in sitting, focusing, and concentrating skills, are minimized with routine. If you are thinking about home-schooling in the future, we believe an infant routine is the starting point for optimum development.

Benefits of PDF for Ryan's Mother

1. A rational response to mothering is natural, since Ryan's basic needs become predictable. Nathan's mom tends to be "strung-out" emotionally. Life is not predictable for her or her son.

2. A mother is not enslaved to her child, since the program allows her to keep life's demands in balance. Nathan's mom is, in a sense, in bondage to his unpredictability.

3. With PDF, a metabolic structure develops that naturally encourages a mother's body to synchronize with her natural rhythmic cycles. That, in turn, enhances successful breast-feeding. In contrast, the nature of demand feeding forces Nathan's mom to many periods of snack feeding. Many moms who feed on demand are so tired that they prematurely give up breast-feeding.

4. Breast-feeding mothers on PDF rarely have problems with their let-down reflex. In contrast, Nathan's mom nurses him so often that sometimes her let down is delayed, frustrating her child; or worse yet, her let down does not occur at all.

5. Because of routine, PDF mothers tend to move back into hormonal balance sooner than non-PDF mothers. Nathan's mom had a terrible bout with postpartum depression. Her condition is not abnormal for mothers whose bodies are worn out from the absence of structure.

6. Ryan's mom not only regains her physical strength quickly, but also returns to her other roles of life, such as wife, daughter, neighbor, and friend. Nathan's mom is often not in the mood for seeing anyone.

7. Overall, Ryan's mom and the other mothers who follow PDF have less maternal anxiety than mothers who choose to demand feed. Much of the guesswork has

been removed with the reliable 24-hour plan. Life becomes very predictable and reassuring.

Benefits of PDF for Ryan's Father

1. PDF encourages fatherly involvement from the beginning. It involves more than offering an occasional bottle and encourages Dad to be active in assessment and decision making. Nathan's dad is not part of the management team.

2. The husband-wife relationship is the cornerstone of the family. From the beginning, both of Ryan's parents have cared for him, not just one of them.

THE BENEFITS OF ROUTINE

In light of the length of time we have with our children until they are grown, an infant feeding plan may not seem very significant. But it is! A plan is the first step to successful parenting. Without one, you will potentially end up like Nathan and his mom.

Parent-directed feeding encourages and enhances the rhythmical needs of your infant. The principles work because they reinforce—not violate—the natural laws of development. PDF is not a prepackaged program, but one you design for the benefit of all your family members. If you follow the basic principles associated with this plan, you will be ready and competent to lovingly direct the life of your child.

QUESTIONS FOR REVIEW

1. What are the two popular misconceptions regarding infant schedules?

2. What is PDF?

3. Describe the difference between Ryan's and Nathan's night-time sleep patterns.

4. What is relational security?

5. How can you easily prove the lack of security in a child that is carried all day in a sling?

4

HUNGER AND SLEEP CYCLES

As listed in the previous chapter, there are many benefits to parent-directed feeding. One of the most obvious is the establishment of stable nighttime sleep patterns. That means your baby sleeps all night along with the rest of the family. Healthy full-term babies are born with the ability to sleep continuously for 7-8 hours through the night and usually within eight weeks. Much of your success will depend on your parenting philosophy and feeding practices.

A number of reasons have been offered in an attempt to explain why some babies sleep through the night early and others do not. The explanations range from simple to complex, from reasonably logical to extremely bizarre. A new mother, speaking from lack of experience, usually provides the simplest comment: "Every child is different. Some can sleep; others cannot." The behavioral clinician may suggest that a child's temperament is the determining influence on sleep patterns: "Some children are easier to handle by nature; some are more difficult." Others may suggest that the need of each child varies: "A high-need baby requires more nocturnal parental interaction; a low-need baby requires less." Although each statement contains a grain of truth, the statements themselves are incomplete.

The feeding pattern you establish with your little one appears to be the key to controlling nighttime sleep behavior. During feeding times, parents have the greatest interaction with their newborn. That interaction triggers a natural cause-and-effect relationship. When Ryan's mom starts out with routine feeding periods, she is actually establishing stable hunger patterns. When these feeding patterns stabilize, nighttime sleep patterns will soon follow suit. When feeding periods are routinely inconsistent, nighttime sleep is not achieved.

ROUTINE FEEDINGS AND NIGHTTIME SLEEP

There is a direct relationship between regular daytime feeding periods and nighttime sleep patterns. Ryan's cousin, Nathan, having been fed on demand, now has great difficulty establishing stable and uninterrupted nighttime sleep. Sometimes he wakes as often as every 2 hours on a recurring basis, and he may do that routinely for two years, according to some studies.[5] That pattern is not healthy for Nathan or his mom. No wonder she seems tired all the time.

Nathan's mom believes that her son's lack of ability to sleep continuously through the night is a result of breast-feeding. She read somewhere that breast-fed babies are not capable of sleeping through the night. Actually, failure to establish continuous nighttime sleep is not associated with breast-feeding, but with demand-feeding (i.e., the lack of routine). Demand-fed babies do not sleep through the night. Ryan and the thousands of other babies on PDF who are breast-fed sleep through the night just fine without injury to successful lactation.

Ryan's mom realizes that continuous nighttime sleep has less to do with the food offered (breast milk or formula) and more to do with the lack of routine. Mothers who demand-feed their babies with formula usually end up with the same unfortunate results.

The feeding philosophy is the starting point in establishing a routine. How a mom meets her child's nutrition needs during the day will either interact positively or negatively with the lower-brain function from which cyclical stabilization takes place. If there is no regularity to feeding, there is no basis for stabilization.

Newborns on PDF establish many restful and continuous periods of sleep. Sometime between the third and the eighth week, Ryan's parents can expect his nighttime sleep cycles to be a continuous 7-8 hours. By three months of age, that time is extended to 10-12 hours each night. This nighttime sleep is in addition to his regular naptimes during the day.

NATURE VERSUS NURTURE

Each feeding philosophy represents a different style of infant management. One is parent-directed, one is child-centered. The contrast in philosophies produces contrasting results.

Although sleep research is still a new frontier in behavioral pediatrics, three facts stand out from our experience.

Fact 1:   Average, healthy, full-term newborns have a pre-disposition for continuous nighttime sleep by the eighth week.

Fact 2:   Newborn sleep cycles cannot stabilize until hunger and digestive patterns are stabilized.

Fact 3: Routine parental interaction stabilizes hunger patterns. Inconsistent parental interaction fosters irregular hunger patterns and thereby creates instability in the child's sleep/wake cycles.

When you consider these facts, especially the last, how should you interact with your newborn in order to achieve optimum development? Follow a basic routine from the beginning. The next consideration is: Who is in the best position to determine that routine—the child or the parent? Nathan's parents wrongly believe that their baby should regulate his own routine and that their job is to respond. After all, a baby knows when he is hungry and when he is ready for sleep. Yes, babies know when they are hungry, but they are not capable of regulating their hunger patterns. Yes, babies know when they are tired, but they are not capable of establishing stable sleep/wake cycles on their own. Parental guidance is necessary.

Parent-directed feeding provides that guidance by establishing a rhythmic structure suited for metabolic stabilization. A newborn needs outward structure until his central nervous system is fully developed. PDF is that outward structure. The principles of PDF work for Ryan because they are directed toward the constant factors of his development, not the variables of his temperament. As his mother provides daily interaction with him through predictable feeding patterns, his hunger and sleep/wake cycles stabilize.

HUNGER PATTERNS
From the point of birth onward, infant hunger patterns will become either stable and regular or unstable and

inconsistent. The determining factor is whether or not you are following a feeding routine with a minimum of 2½ hours from the end of the last feeding to the beginning of the next. When infants are fed on the PDF plan, their hunger patterns stabilize. The reason for this stabilization is that the hunger mechanism (digestion and absorption) operates as if it has a metabolic memory that is reinforced by routine. If Ryan's feeding periods are regular, he will establish a hunger metabolism that is stable and predictable. For example, if his mom feeds him at approximately 7:00 a.m., 10:00 a.m., 1:00 p.m., 4:00 p.m., 7:00 p.m., and 10:00 p.m., his hunger metabolism will begin to line up to those times. But that happens only when the feeding periods are routine. As his hunger metabolism stabilizes, his digestive metabolism stabilizes.

In contrast, erratic feeding periods confuse an infant's young memory. Since the parental response changes from day to day, often hour to hour, there is no chance for the hunger mechanism to stabilize. With the way Nathan is being fed, any programmed stability will be a matter of chance. That is why Nathan will probably take two years before he sleeps through the night and why he is a candidate for sleep-related problems in childhood.

Is Infant Sleep Deprivation Dangerous?

Imagine what would happen to an adult who was not allowed to sleep more than 3 hours on average for one week. The negative effects to his mature central nervous system are well established. But what about an infant whose central nervous system is still developing? Our question then is: To what extent does sleep deprivation negatively impact an infant's developing central nervous system? Imagine parenting in such a way that your baby is not allowed to sleep continuously for eight hours, even one night out of three-hundred and sixty-five. Could many of the learning disabilities associated with a nonstructured approach to parenting be rooted in something as basic as the absence of continuous nights of sleep in the first year of life when the higher brain is still developing?

SLEEP/WAKE CYCLES

Because Ryan is under the influence of parent-directed feeding, he will tend to establish many more restful periods than his cousin. In the early months, an infant sleeps most of the time. Half of this sleep time is spent in quiet sleep (relaxed sleep pattern, or RSP) and the other half in active sleep (active sleep pattern, or ASP). Researchers tell us these two patterns alternate about every 30-45 minutes during sleep time.

There are noticeable differences between these two patterns. During the relaxed sleep state, you will see a more peaceful baby. His face is relaxed, his eyelids are closed and still, and he has very few body movements. His breathing is quiet and very regular.

The active sleep state is a more restless state. In both children and adults, this is our dream state. The extent to which infants dream is not yet known. During this period, the arms and legs stir, the eyes and mouth flutter, and facial activities such as sucking, frowning, and chewing motions occur. Breathing is irregular and slightly faster.

How do ASP and RSP relate to feeding patterns in the first twelve weeks? Although Nathan experiences some RSP, he fails to experience the cycle on a continual basis. From the start, he has been put to the breast 10-15 times a day and allowed to suckle for 45 minutes to an hour. With that type of feeding pattern, there is not much time left for the RSP cycle to repeat itself. Nathan's nights are much like his days: a series of naps between feedings.

On the other hand, Ryan experiences the necessary

length of sleep for the RSP/ASP cycle to naturally repeat itself because of the basic routine set up by his parents.

HINDRANCES TO CONTINUOUS NIGHTTIME SLEEP
Where there is the ability, there is the capacity. The average infant has both the natural ability and capacity to sleep through the night sometime within the first two months of life. It is an acquired skill enhanced by routine.

The pathology of sleep deprivation in infants and toddlers has much less to do with *nature* than with *nurture*. Sleep is a natural function of the body. The primary cue for infant sleep is sleepiness. Sleep cues are influenced (often negatively) by a variety of sleep association props. Some sleep props, such as a special blanket or stuffed animal, are harmless, while others are addictive. For some, the problem is getting the child to fall asleep initially. For others, the problem is getting the child to fall back to sleep without a prop once prematurely awakened. In addition to what we listed above (i.e., lack of routine feedings), the three most common negative sleep props are:

1. intentionally nursing a baby to sleep
2. rocking a baby to sleep
3. shared sleep (sleeping with a baby)

Intentionally Nursing Your Baby to Sleep

The question is not whether you should nurse your baby, but whether it is an appropriate method of sleep control. We believe the answer is no. Such sleep cues only create an unnecessary sleep dependency.

The scenario is all too familiar. A mother nurses her baby to sleep. Slowly lifting herself from the chair, she begins moving toward the crib. Holding her breath, she gently puts the baby down. Then, frozen for a moment, she anxiously waits for peace to settle over the crib. She backs up to the door in hopes of making her escape. If the baby fusses, the process begins all over.

There is a much better way than being in bondage to your baby's sleep needs. A routine allows infants to establish healthy sleep patterns and to be put down in the crib awake.

Rocking Your Baby to Sleep

Once again, the issue is not whether you rock or cuddle your baby. We trust that happens regularly. But are you creating sleep props that interfere with your child's ability to initially fall asleep or to fall back asleep when prematurely awakened?

Akin to rocking a baby to sleep are the modern mechanical sleep props such as the clothes dryer. (Yes, the clothes dryer!) It was discovered that the dryer creates enough vibration to lull a baby to sleep. Another method is the naptime or nighttime car ride. The sound of the motor and the vibrating chassis sends the baby to sleepland. Both approaches work, temporarily. That is, they work until the dryer runs out of time, the car runs out of gas, or you run out of patience.

Sleeping with Your Baby

The most serious security-related sleep problems we counsel are those associated with parents who sleep with their babies. Sharing sleep with children puts them at risk both physically and emotionally. Physically, rolling on top of the child and smothering him to death is a real threat.[6] Such infant deaths are labeled parental overlay and are just now receiving the media attention they deserve.

Emotionally, this method is passively abusive. It can create a state of abnormal dependency on the sleep prop to the point that the child actually fears falling asleep when transitioned to his own bed. As the child moves into toddlerhood, he expresses that fear through the need for his parent to lie down with him at naptime until he falls asleep. In several of our recovery cases, toddlers used vomiting as a coping mechanism to draw the parent to their presence. Others rhythmically bang their heads against the wall. Shared sleep creates a false sense of security. Too often children cannot function outside the parent's presence, since their security is based on proximity, not relationship.

We believe that sleeping with your baby in the long run creates needs and does not prevent them. The real question is, Why use sleep association props in the first place, when a basic routine will naturally enhance restful sleep? If you put your baby to bed awake, he will establish longer and stronger sleep cycles than if you put him down already asleep. None of the sleep manipulation methods listed offer any healthy advantages. You must think of the long-term effects. Do not create a behavior that will later call for retraining. Feed your baby, rock him and love him, but put him down before he falls asleep. (See Chapter 10 for an expanded discussion on the family-bed theory.)

SUMMARY

Which feeding philosophy will you follow with your newborn? The one you choose will ultimately influence your child's sleep patterns. Remember, a contrast in approach produces a contrast in results—either sleepless nights or peaceful rest for baby, Mom, and the rest of the family.

QUESTIONS FOR REVIEW

1. Explain how feeding patterns influence nighttime sleep behavior.

2. What are three facts that relate to infant sleep?

   a.

   b.

   c.

3. Should you allow your baby to regulate his own routine? Explain your answer.

4. How do erratic feeding periods confuse an infant's young memory?

5. What is a sleep prop?

6. List the three hindrances to nighttime sleep.

   a.

   b.

   c.

5

FACTS ON FEEDING

How you feed your baby is perhaps the most basic task of infant management. Since a baby's sucking and rooting reflexes are well developed at birth, he will satisfy those reflexes by rooting and sucking on anything near his mouth. Whether feeding is done by a bottle or the breast is not as important as the gentle and tender cuddling you give him during feeding.

Your decision to bottle- or breast-feed must be free of any coercion or manipulation. You will make the right decision when you are best informed. There is no question from both medical and popular opinions that breast-feeding is most preferred for its physiological benefits. A mother's milk is a complete and perfect food. It is easily digested, provides excellent nutrition, and contains the right balance of proteins and fats. It also provides additional antibodies that are necessary for establishing your baby's early immune system.[7]

Breast-feeding has advantages for Mom as well. It helps speed the return of her uterus to its normal size and shape. It is also the most economical and convenient way

to feed her baby. There is no cleanup, storing, or heating needed, and there is nothing to pack away when you travel. While stored in the breast, the milk never spoils or gets too old to use.

Transforming a woman into a good mother is one accomplishment breast-feeding cannot achieve. There is no "good-mother" hormone, and much more is required than just bringing a baby to breast. We believe strongly in breast-feeding but do not believe in breast-feeding at all cost. That last statement is in need of further clarification.

If breast-feeding and breast-milk production were the only categories of developmental interest to new parents, and the primary category of child development, then there would be no need for this book, nor would there be so many parents looking for help. We differ from the demand/attachment style of parenting starting with our premises. We do not believe that breast-feeding itself is the genesis of development nor the basis of psychological health. Where breast-feeding ranks in relationship to other developmental categories appears to be the fundamental difference between the routine and nonroutine approaches to parenting. It is not the importance of breast feeding that is in question but which method of breast-feeding, (demand versus PDF) can best complement the overall advancement of the child in all critical areas of development.

In the Chapter 3, we compared the developmental success of the two approaches relating to early training of infants, pretoddlers, and toddlers. We contrasted the accomplishments in the areas of taking naps, continuous nighttime sleep, characterization of fussiness and contentment dispositions, signs of insecurity, family attachment as compared to mother attachment, the ratio percentage of "high-need" babies, sitting, focusing, and concentrating skills, self-play adeptness, problem-solving skills, ability to

yield to parental direction, learning disability propensities, and any other category basic to the first two years of life. Since success in all those categories is more important to us than the single category of lactation, and since there is more to good parenting than successful lactation, we do not believe in breast-feeding at all costs. There may come a time when going to the bottle rather than some breast-feeding extreme is the most loving thing a mother can do for her baby. Both bottle- and breast-feeding provide opportunity to cuddle, care, and love. Bottle-feeding and formula are discussed in more detail in the latter sections of this chapter.

MILK PRODUCTION

If breast-feeding is your choice, there are a few basic principles to understand. Most important is that breast-feeding is based on a demand-and-supply basis (not to be confused with the economic principle of supply and demand). The supply of milk produced by the glands is proportionate to the demand placed on the system.

Nathan's mother was told that her milk production was directly related to the number of feedings she offered—the more feedings, the greater the milk production. The theory that quantitative feedings equal quantitative milk production is inaccurate. There is some truth in that statement, but the statement as a whole is not true.

Certainly a mother who takes her baby to breast 5 times a day will produce more milk than the one who offers only one feeding. However, there are limits. A mother who takes her baby to her breast 12, 15, or 20 times a day will not produce any more milk than the mom who takes her baby to breast 6-7 times a day.

The difference between the two moms is *qualitative* feeding versus *quantitative* feedings. With qualitative feeding, you eliminate the need for quantitative snacking. And that is exactly what many feedings become—a snack, not a meal. The opinion that many feedings automatically equate to maximized milk production is a common misunderstanding. We counsel many mothers who do poorly as a result of unlimited feedings. Successful breast-feeding includes more factors than just bringing the baby to the breast frequently.

Part of a mother's ability to produce milk is tied to the demand placed on her system. Two factors associated with the demand side of breast-milk production are: the appropriate *stimulation* at each feeding and the *time* between each feeding. Without proper stimulation, no matter how many times an infant goes to the breast, milk production will be limited. Too many snack feedings (too little time between feedings) may reduce proper stimulation; not enough feedings (too much time between feedings) reduces milk production. Time and stimulation are interrelated and are necessary for successful breast-feeding.

When we speak of breast stimulation, we are referring to the intensity of the suck. The hunger drive is a consistent influence on the sucking reflex. This drive is associated with the time it takes for an infant to digest and absorb the milk. The infant who is fed on a basic 3-hour routine and whose digestive metabolism is stabilized will demand more milk, thereby stimulating greater milk production as compared to the child who feeds more often but demands less. Again, the issue is hunger feeding versus snack feeding.

For example, the newborn who feeds every 1½ hours will stimulate only enough milk to meet that need. That is why demand-fed babies feed more often—they snack more often. They are not getting a complete meal, but a partial one. That may also be the reason so many new mothers get discouraged and give up breast-feeding so quickly; feeding is practically all they do around the clock.

On the other hand, an infant nursing every 3 hours will signal for greater milk production. Since the need is greater, the supply is increased. Because the supply is increased, the baby goes longer between feedings.

As a general guide, for the first two months you will not feed less than 2½ hours **from the end of the last feeding to the start of the next**, and no more often than every 3 to 3½ hours. Sooner than 2½ hours can wear Mom down, often causing a decrease in milk production. Waiting more that 3½ hours to feed fails to produce the stimulation needed for a sufficient quantity of milk. (Feeding 2½ hours from the end of the last feeding equates to a 3-hour routine once you add the 20 to 30 minutes required for the next feeding.)

THE LET-DOWN REFLEX

When a baby begins to suckle on his mother's breast, a message is sent to her pituitary gland, which in turn releases several hormones. Necessary for milk production is the hormone prolactin and for milk release is the hormone oxytocin. The most important factor in the continued release of prolactin is proper nipple stimulation. Without proper stimulation, milk will not be produced no matter how many times an infant goes to the breast. A continuous routine will help maximize milk production.

Oxytocin causes the muscles around the milk glands to contract, forcing milk into the ducts. When that happens, it is said that the milk has been "let down." Some mothers experience a tingling or pressure sensation at the point of let down. Without this reflex, the milk would stay in the glands.

The milk that is released is called the *hindmilk,* or mature milk. This high-protein and high-fat content milk is rich in calories (30-40 per ounce). Before the milk is let down, your baby will receive a milk substance stored in the ducts under the areola (the flesh encircling the nipples). This *foremilk*, as it is called, is more diluted and limited in nutritional value.

Mothers following PDF have little or no problem with the let-down reflex compared to those who demand-feed. There are two reasons for that. First, routine plays an important part in proper let down. Not only does the mind need a routine to maintain order and efficiency, but the body does as well. The very nature of inconsistent feeding wears on a woman's body.

A second reason is the high confidence level of the mother who follows a routine. For her, there is no need to question or second guess what will happen next. She is confident and her confidence aids the successful working of her let-down reflex. In fact, because of her routine, she is much more in tune with her baby and his needs. She knows intuitively when something is wrong because it falls so obviously outside the norm of her baby's behavior. In contrast, the lack of confidence that comes with the absence of routine only produces worrisome fear and anxiety (fear in not knowing if the baby received enough at the last feeding; anxiety in not knowing what to do next). There is no "norm" for these mothers. That is what further perpetuates the anxiety cycle. Such anxiety can impact a mother to the extent that she does not let down her milk at all.

BREAST MILK AND BABY'S DIGESTION

Does an empty stomach trigger the hunger drive? No. The purpose of digestion is to break down the various food groups into proteins, fats, and carbohydrates. The end product of digestion is absorption. Absorption, which takes place primarily in the small intestine, is the process by which the broken-down food molecules pass through the intestinal lining into the bloodstream. As absorption is accomplished, the blood-sugar level drops. That drop, in turn, sends a signal to the hypothalamus gland calling for more food. A drop in blood sugar, not an empty stomach, is the signal for more food.

Breast milk is digested faster than formula, but that fact does not justify unlimited feedings. The comparison should not be made between using breast milk and formula but instead by the amount of breast milk consumed at each feeding. Demand-fed babies tend to snack all day. PDF babies have a complete meal at each feeding.

The child who nurses frequently and takes in fewer ounces of milk will naturally be hungry more often. In contrast, the child on PDF takes in more ounces, thereby causing the digestive and absorption processes to take longer.

NURSING YOUR NEW BABY

During the first few days of nursing, find a comfortable position in which to nurse, possibly using a pillow under your supporting arm to lessen the stress on your neck and upper back. Begin with 3-7 minutes on each breast. That time frame will allow for sufficient nipple stimulation.

Do not be discouraged if your baby does not catch on right away; he will not starve. Your baby is born with sufficient water and extra calories to sustain him until your milk comes in, usually between three and six days. During that period, some weight loss in the baby is normal and should be expected. By twelve to fourteen days, your baby should have regained his birth weight. It is important that you learn to listen to how well your baby swallows. That signal, along with five to seven wet diapers per day, is a good indicator that your baby is getting enough milk to grow on.

The first milk produced is a thick, yellowish liquid

called colostrum. Colostrum is high in protein (at least 5 times as high as mature milk) and has less fat and sugar than later milk. It is a protein concentrate that takes longer to digest and is rich in antibodies. Occasionally some mothers experience tenderness in the first few days before their milk comes in. That is due to the thickness of the colostrum and the infant exerting more negative pressure to remove it. His pattern is suck, suck, suck, then swallow. Once your milk comes in, your baby will respond with a rhythmic swallow, suck, swallow, suck, swallow, suck, swallow. At that point, the negative pressure is reduced, and the tenderness goes away.

Positioning Your Baby

Proper positioning is essential to successful nursing. When the baby nurses, he should take both the nipple and all or much of the areola into his mouth. Encourage the baby to latch on to the areola. With correct positioning, your baby's entire torso is already facing you. With your nipple, stroke lightly and downward on his lower lip until he opens his mouth. (Be careful not to touch his upper lip.) When his mouth opens wide, center your nipple and pull him close to you so the tip of his nose is touching your breast and his knees are touching your abdomen.

Successful latching on is made difficult if the baby's body is opened away from the mother's abdomen, but his head is turned toward the breast. That position is wrong. When the baby is correctly latched on, nursing will not be painful. If there is discomfort, remove him and relatch him.

A nursing baby often has a remarkably strong suck. If you try to pull the nipple away, he will just suckle harder. To remove him without hurting yourself, slip your little finger between the corner of his mouth and your breast.

That will break the suction, allowing you to take him off easily.

THE NURSING PERIOD

Once your milk is established, you should nurse 10-15 minutes on a side for a total of 20-30 minutes, or use the 7-7-7-7 method, alternating each breast after 7 minutes with burping in between. That method is especially helpful when you have a sleepy baby to assure that both breasts are stimulated.

The maximum time per side normally will not exceed 15 minutes. Studies show that in established lactation, the breasts can be emptied in 7-10 minutes per side, providing the infant is sucking vigorously. By pointing out that fact, we are not encouraging less time at the breast but showing just how much can be accomplished in a short amount of time.

If you are spending 30 minutes to 1 hour at a time nursing or feeding a healthy baby, there may be too much playing taking place. If you feel your baby has a need for nonnutritive sucking, a pacifier can meet the need without compromising the benefits of your routine. Successful breast-feeding mothers feel confident about when and how long to feed their babies.

BREAST VERSUS BOTTLE

When it comes to infant nutrition, mother's milk is clearly superior to formula. But what about when it comes to nurturing? Which is best, breast or bottle? In times past, writers stressed the value of breast-feeding and labeled bottle-feeding as a way of rejecting a child and as a sign that the mother lacks warmth. Some have said that she is renouncing her biological role as a woman and her emotional role as a mother. Others considered bottle-fed children to have less of an advantage than those breast-fed.

Actually, studies over the last sixty years that attempted to correlate the method of infant feeding with emotional development in later life have failed to support any such conclusion. A mother's attitude toward her child as expressed in the total context of parenting is more important than any one isolated factor, such as the manner of feeding.

BOTTLE-FEEDING

Bottle-feeding is not a twentieth-century discovery, but a practice that has been around thousands of years. Our ancestors made bottles out of wood, porcelain, pewter, glass, copper, leather, and cow horns. Historically, unprocessed animal's milk was the principal nourishment used with bottle-feeding. Because the milk was easily contaminated, infant mortality was high.

When bottle-feeding was in fashion during the first half of this century, one size fit all. But today your grocer's shelves are filled with options. Besides the standardized glass and plastic bottles from which to choose, there are those with disposable bags, designer styles, handles, and even animal shapes. All of these choices come in a vast array of colors and prints.

To add to a mother's confusion is the selection of the proper nipple. You can select anything from a nursing nipple that is most like Mom to an orthodontic nipple. There are juice, formula, water, and even cereal nipples. Actually, the most important consideration is to make sure you purchase a nipple that has the right-sized hole. Too large a hole causes the child to drink too fast. Excessive spitting up and projectile vomiting can be signs of overly rapid fluid intake. A hole that is too small creates a hungry and discontented child. These simple tips will prevent what may seem to be major feeding problems with your baby.[8]

Bottle-feeding allows others to participate. Feeding

time for Dad is just as special to him, and he should not be denied the opportunity to participate. The same is true with grandparents, brothers, and sisters. Raising children is a family affair. Keep it that way.

FORMULA

If bottle-feeding is your choice, take the time to sit down and hold your baby during feeding times. You need the rest and your baby needs the cuddling. Also, holding your baby will help prevent your child from becoming attached to the bottle, since he alone will not be in control of his eating.

As a general rule, you should not feed your baby while he or she is lying completely flat, such as when the mother is nursing in the lying down position. It is postulated that swallowing while lying down allows nasopharyngeal fluid to enter the middle ear leading to subsequent infection. Avoid propping the bottle up for the same reasons. We also caution mothers not to put an older child (six months and up) to bed with a bottle. This is true not only for health factors relating to ear infections but also for oral hygiene. When a child falls asleep with a bottle in his mouth, the sugar in the formula left in the mouth coats the teeth, causing tooth decay.

The most important decision you will make about bottle-feeding is what to put inside the bottle. Some of the choices will be made for you either by the hospital in which you deliver or by your pediatrician. If either you or your husband has a history of milk allergies, mention it to your doctor. That may influence the type of formula the pediatrician recommends.

Today's formulas have properties closely matched to those of breast milk, including the proper balance and quantity of proteins, fats, and carbohydrates. Cow's milk and baby formula are not the same. Formula is designed for a baby's digestive system; cow's milk is not and should not be given to a child less than a year old. Check with your pediatrician or your hospital for more information regarding the different manufacturers of formula.

The amount of formula taken at each feeding will vary with age. The average, as with breast-fed babies, is anywhere from 1½ to 3 ounces per feeding in the first several weeks, with a gradual increase as the child grows. If you prepare a 4-ounce bottle for each feeding and allow your baby to take as much as he wants, he will tend to stop when he has enough. Keep in mind that a larger baby might take more milk, but not necessarily. As with breast-fed babies, the feeding routine is what establishes the corresponding hunger patterns and not the substance or the amount of food.

Formula-fed babies need to be burped after every ½ ounce at first. By the time your baby is between four and six months old, he will probably be able to take the full 6-8 ounces before burping. With both breast-feeding and bottle-feeding, there is a certain amount of spitting up that takes place. When that happens, there is no cause for alarm. However, if you find your infant rejecting all his food frequently, contact your pediatrician.

Breast milk is the best form of infant nourishment. But if you choose not to nurse, or if you decide to discontinue nursing within the first twelve months, that decision in no way reflects upon your status as a mother. Just as breast-feeding does not make you a good mother, bottle-feeding does not make you a bad one.

QUESTIONS FOR REVIEW

1. What is the difference between qualitative and quantitative feedings?

2. What two factors influence breast milk production? Explain your answer.

3. List seven ways to determine if your baby is getting enough nutrition.

   a.

   b.

   c.

   d.

e.

f.

g.

4. List the four reasons for poor latching on.

   a.

   b.

   c.

   d.

5. True or False: There is no relationship between the method of infant feeding (breast vs. bottle) and later personality development.

6

MONITORING YOUR
BABY'S GROWTH

One of the many advantages to PDF is the success mothers have with breast-feeding. Having the knowledge that her baby's nutritional needs will be met in an orderly fashion is freeing to any woman. Under the PDF plan, there is no need for guesswork or for attempting to overcompensate by offering unlimited feedings. But there is a need for caution.

Being on a routine does not eliminate the possibility of lactation problems. Those problems do not stem from a 2½- to 3-hour routine but the variables influencing your routine and attempts to breast-feed. Those variables include proper sleep, diet, nutrition, state of mind, age of mother, first child or sixth, her desire and physical capacity to breast-feed, nursing techniques, and the baby's ability to properly latch on. This chapter will survey some basic precautions for breast-feeding mothers that will assure healthy growth and development for their babies.

SIGNS OF ADEQUATE NUTRITION

If you are breast feeding, how do you know if your baby is getting enough food? Ask yourself:

1. Is my baby sleeping well between feedings?
2. Is my baby gaining weight and/or growing in length?
3. Is my baby's urine clear (not very yellow)?
4. Is my baby alert and responsive during waketime?
5. Is my baby's mouth moist (not dry)?
6. Is my baby having five to seven wet diapers per day (some of them saturated)?
7. Does my baby appear content (but not sluggish) after feeding?

A "yes" answer to these questions implies your baby is getting enough food. If you suspect that something is not right, contact your pediatrician. He is the first medical authority in your baby's life, and you are responsible to be discerning.

Weight Gain Concerns

If your child is not gaining weight or is acting sluggish, contact your pediatrician. Those symptoms need to be investigated. With the conservative practice of PDF, weight gain will be steady and continuous. We routinely monitor the progress of PDF babies and continue to find wonderful results. In our most recent survey, we randomly examined the charts of thirty babies—twenty-eight breast-fed and two bottle-fed. Length and weight gains were measured at one, four, eight, and sixteen weeks. All babies were sleeping through the night by week eight.

When compared against national pediatric norms, on average the girls fell into the 72% range with continuous growth, and 54% in weight. Of the sixteen boys surveyed, their length was recorded at 61% of the national average and weight at 56% with continuous growth. Among the boys, the average birth weight registered at 44% of the national norms. By the fourth month their weight gain on PDF placed them at 63% of the norms. This does not represent a scientific study, but it does represent the norm for PDF babies. A basic routine does not detract from proper weight gain.

Low birth-weight babies do well on a conservative routine. Although some newborns start off at the low end of the national norms, they continue to gain weight in proportion to the genetic potential for stature inherited from their parents. That is, smaller parents usually give birth to smaller babies, thus weight gain will usually be proportionately less. Add the weight gain benefits to sleeping through the night, and the greater benefits of PDF are quickly realized.

Weight-Gain Guide

Birth to Two Weeks:
Approximate average: Regain birth weight.

Two Weeks to Three Months:
Approximate average: 2 pounds per month or 1 ounce per day.

Four to Six Months:
Approximate average: 1 pound per month or ½ ounce per day. (At six months, the baby should have doubled his birth weight.)

One Year:
Approximate average: 2½ to 3 times his birth weight.

Failure to Thrive Babies

There is a difference between slow weight gain and "failure to thrive." With the first, weight gain is slow but consistent. In contrast, failure to thrive describes an infant who continues to lose weight after ten days of life, does not regain his birth weight by three weeks of age, or gains at an unusually slow rate beyond a month. The cause of slow or absent weight gain can be attributed to both mother and child.

There are several maternal causes for slow or absent weight gain.

1. Improper nursing technique. It is amazing how many women fail at breast-feeding due to improper positioning of the baby on the breast. Latching-on problems are commonly the result of:

   Wrong Positioning. This means the baby is not positioned properly on the breast. As a result, some babies latch on only to the nipple and not all or much of the areola. The end result is a hungry baby.

2. Nature or lifestyle. Insufficient milk production can be a result of nature (insufficient glandular tissue) or a mother's lifestyle (not getting enough rest or liquids). She simply does not produce enough milk.

3. Poor release of milk. This indicates a problem with the mother's let-down reflex.

4. Too many feedings. Ironically, one would think that many feedings would ensure adequate weight gain. Not necessarily! In some cases a mother can be worn out by too many ineffective feedings. When we first

met Jeffrey, he was six weeks old and had only gained one pound. The breast was offered each time he cried, approximately every 1 to 1½-hours. The baby was properly latched on. Jeffrey's mother simply was fatigued. Although he was failing to thrive, the only counsel this mother received was to feed more often and sling her baby. In contrast, we put her on a 3-hour routine. Her poor health necessitated a formula complement. In a few days, the starving child started to gain weight. In a week, he was sleeping through the night. Jeffrey's mother successfully breast-fed his subsequent siblings on the PDF plan without a weight-gain problem.

5. Infrequent feedings. This problem can be attributed to both hyperscheduling or demand feeding. The mother that insists on watching the clock to the minute lacks confidence in decision making. The clock is in control, not the parent. Some demand-fed babies request food too infrequently, thus not sufficiently stimulating the breast for adequate milk production. Routine feedings with a time limitation between feedings eliminate this problem. That is why neonatal and intensive care units stay close to a 3-hour feeding schedule. It ensures adequate nutrition in a timely fashion. It's healthy!

There are also several infant causes for slow or no weight gain.

1. A weak suck. In this case, the child does not have the coordination or the strength to suck properly, remain latched on, or activate the let-down reflex. As a result the baby receives the low-calorie foremilk but not the high-calorie hindmilk.

2. Improper suckling. This can result from a number of

different conditions.

a. <u>Tongue thrusting</u>. When going to breast, some babies thrust their tongues forward and push the nipple out of their mouth.

b. <u>Tongue tied.</u> Latching on is made difficult when the *frenulum* (the tissue that attaches the tongue to the floor of the mouth) is too short or is attached too close to the front of the tongue.

c. <u>Protruding tongue</u>. This condition is described as the tongue forming a hump in the mouth, interfering with successful latching on.

d. <u>Tongue sucking.</u> The infant suckles his own tongue.

3. An underlying medical problem. A weak or laborious suck, one in which the child tires to the point of giving up after a few minutes of nursing, can be a symptom of cardiac or neurological failing. If you suspect this may be the case, do not wait for your baby's next scheduled checkup. Call your pediatrician immediately.

There are many variables involved in successful breast-milk production, but fortunately, your baby's routine is a positive one.

NOTE: Breast-feeding proficiency is usually a matter of standard review in childbirth classes. For additional help, consider taking a breast-feeding class at your local hospital or rent a "how-to" video. You can attend a class and learn proper techniques of breast-feeding without accepting the instructor's personal parenting philosophies. If you are concerned about your progress after your baby arrives, ask your pediatrician to observe your nursing techniques or recommend a lactation educator or consultant.

INSUFFICIENT MILK PRODUCTION

Regardless of which feeding philosophy you follow, you cannot add to what nature has left out. The anxiety created by the fear of failure is itself a contributor to milk deficiency. Because so much guilt is placed on mothers who are not successful at breast-feeding, many of them go to extremes to become milk sufficient.

In most cultures, 5% of nursing mothers during peacetime (up to 10% during war or other stress time) will not produce enough milk to satisfy their infants' needs. Some mothers may initially be milk sufficient but reach a low ceiling by the third month. That ceiling could happen to a mother even though her baby is cooperative and sucking frequently, and she herself is using correct nursing techniques and is receiving sufficient food, rest, and sympathy.

Unfortunately, in our society's rush to get back to nature, we have inadvertently created a perfect-mother stereotype—a "super mom" who endlessly carries her infant, has 12 free hours a day to nurse, and possesses an endless supply of milk. That distorted image of motherhood only creates a stigma of negligence when a mother fails to measure up to the image.

How cruel to put this picture before the 5% of mothers who do their best, but for reasons out of their control, are not milk-sufficient. A woman's ability to lactate and the length of her lactation are not valid measurements of good mothering. Yet some women find their mothering identity in the act of breast-feeding itself. In practice, this elevates the relationship between the mother's breasts and her child above the relationship between the mother herself and her child. For these women, there is an inordinate preoccupation with breast-feeding—anytime, anywhere, for any reason. In such cases a mother may become dependent on breast-feeding to maintain her identity. Be careful. There is more to nurturing a baby than responding with the breast to his every cry.

Testing Your Milk Supply

If you approach the end of the third week and observe a routine fussiness after every feeding, or your baby is having difficulty going 2½ to 3 hours on mother's milk, review the external stresses in your life and try to eliminate what you can. Are you too busy, not getting enough liquids or enough sleep? Is your calorie intake adequate? Are you following your doctor's recommendation for supplemental vitamins during lactation? Are you consuming too many dairy products? Also consider the technical aspects associated with feeding. Is the baby positioned properly and latched on correctly?

If you find your baby is still not content after checking all external factors, consider trying one or both of the following tests.

1. Consider feeding your baby five to seven days on a strict 2½-hour routine. If your milk production increases (as demonstrated by your baby becoming more content and sleeping better), work your way back to the 3-hour minimum. If no improvement comes, work back to 3 hours with the aid of a formula complement for the benefit of your baby and for your own peace of mind.

2. The four-day test involves offering a complementary feeding of 1-2 ounces of formula after each nursing period. Then express your milk, manually or with a breast pump (electric pump preferably), 10 minutes per side. Keep track of how much extra you are producing. If your milk is plentiful, then the problem lies with your baby. He is either not latching on properly, or he is a lazy nurser. If your milk supply increases as a result of pumping, which will be indicated either by milk expressed or by your baby not wanting the complementary feeding, then return to breast-feeding only, maintaining a 3-hour routine.

   If the additional stimulation via pumping does not increase your milk supply, and if you reviewed all the external factors and found them compatible with nursing, then you are probably part of the 5% mentioned earlier. The solution is not found in more nursing, sleeping with your baby, or carrying him around all day. We recommend you use formula and maintain your routine.

QUESTIONS FOR REVIEW

1. Out of a number of possibilities, list at least five variables affecting successful breast-feeding.

   a.

   b.

   c.

   d.

   e.

2. List the seven signs of adequate nutrition.

   a.

   b.

   c.

   d.

   e.

   f.

   g.

3. Describe the difference between slow weight gain and "failure to thrive" babies.

4. Latching-on problems are commonly the result of what? Explain.

5. As it relates to the cause of slow weight gain for an infant, what is weak sucking? List some of the causes.

6. What is a symptom of an underlying medical problem? Describe the condition.

7

ESTABLISHING YOUR BABY'S ROUTINE

Whether you have one baby, twins, or a set of triplets, you begin establishing your routine from day one. Your baby's routine is a 24-hour strategy designed to meet his needs as well as those of the rest of the family.

The strategy we recommend is made up of three basic activities that repeat themselves throughout the day: feeding time, waketime, and naptime. Feeding must be first, waketime second, and naptime third. Do not change that order, with the exception of the late-night and the middle-of-the-night feedings when a waketime is not necessary.

As stated in Chapter 3, the first application of your parenting philosophy will show up in the way you choose to feed your baby. During those moments of nurturing, you are doing more than just filling up a little tummy; you are integrating life into your child and your child into life. This process requires a plan. Whether nourishment is passed on by breast or bottle, the guidelines for success are listed below.

Your baby's first year is divided into four basic phases. phase one: *Stabilization;* phase two: *Extended Night*; phase three: *Extended Day*; and phase four: *Extended Routine*. In this chapter, our focus will be confined to feeding times and related activities associated with each phase. In the next chapter, we will focus on waketime activities and naptime.

Phase One
STABILIZATION
Birth through Eight Weeks

During the first ten days to two weeks, the daily routine for most new mothers will be a continual repeat of a 2½- to 3-hour cycle from the end of one feeding to the beginning of the next. Your schedule should look something like this:

```
|---Feeding---| |--- Wake ---| |------------------ Nap ------------------|
     Time          Time                      Time

|----15-----30----45---- | ----15-----30----45---- | ----15-----30----45---|
     Hour 1                    Hour 2                    Hour 3
```

There are basic goals to achieve during this phase for both Mom and baby. For the breast-feeding mother, the establishment and stabilizing of milk production is the main objective. For the baby, the stabilization of hunger metabolism and sleep/wake cycles are the goals. Another goal may be teaching your baby how to nurse. By the end of the eighth week, he should be sleeping through the night (7-8 hours).

One caution we offer new parents is to be aware that their newborn will tend to fall asleep at the breast before he is done nursing. The parent's job is to keep him awake until feeding is over. Rub his toes, change his diaper, or talk to him. Work on trying to keep him awake until after the feeding period is completed.

A baby's day is divided into four segments:

Morning	**6:00 a.m. - 11:00 a.m.**
Early morning	6:00 a.m. - 9:00 a.m.
Late morning	9:00 a.m. - 11:00 a.m.
Afternoon	**11:00 a.m. - 6:00 p.m.**
Early afternoon	11:00 a.m. - 1:00 p.m.
Midafternoon	1:00 p.m. - 3:00 p.m.
Late afternoon	3:00 p.m. - 6:00 p.m.
Evening	**6:00 p.m. - 11:00 p.m.**
Early evening	6:00 p.m. - 8:00 p.m.
Midevening	8:00 p.m. - 10:00 p.m.
Late evening	10:00 p.m. - 11:00 p.m.
Nighttime	**11:00 p.m. - 6:00 a.m.**

GENERAL GUIDELINES

Do not underestimate the following six guidelines. Although simple, they will bring order to your life and will make you a confident and competent parent.

1. The time between feedings can be measured from the beginning of one feeding to the beginning of the next, or from the end of one feeding to the end of the next. For example, a 3-hour feeding cycle means that 3 hours elapse from the beginning of one feeding period to the beginning of the next. (As previously stated, practically, a 3-hour routine means you will feed your

baby 2½ hours from the end of the previous feeding. When you add in the next 20 to 30 minutes for feeding, you complete the 3-hour cycle.)

2. Starting with the early morning feeding and continuing through the midevening feeding, all three activities will take place: feeding time, waketime, naptime. But during the nighttime segment, there should be no extended wake periods. Feed your baby and put him right back to bed.

3. For the first four to five weeks:

Starting with your early morning feeding and continuing through the midevening feeding, the usual time between each nursing period should be **no less than 2½ hours from the end of one nursing period to the beginning of the next.** Any time increment between the 2½-hour mark and 3 hours is acceptable. During these early weeks, you should stay close to these recommended times. These routine feedings will help to establish and stabilize both lactation and your baby's metabolism.

> **NOTE:** If you need to awaken your baby during the day to prevent him from sleeping longer than the 3½-hour cycle, do so! Such parental intervention is necessary to help stabilize the baby's digestive metabolism. The exception to this guideline comes with the late-evening feeding. There is no need to awaken your baby during the night. Let him wake naturally and then feed him and put him back to bed.

4. Between weeks five and eight:

Starting with your early morning feeding and continuing through the midevening feeding, the usual time between each nursing period should be **no less than 2½ hours and no more than 3½ hours from the end of the last feeding to the start of the next.** Any time increment between those two periods is acceptable.

5. When you establish your baby's routine, first consider all your routine activities, such as grocery shopping, work, exercise, household chores, and church attendance. There will be times when your baby's routine will change to fit into your schedule. At other times you will plan your activity around your baby's needs, simply because it is more practical to do so.

6. Determine the time of the first feeding of the day. That time will be fairly consistent each day and may initially be set by both you and your baby.

SUMMARY OF PHASE ONE

By the end of eight weeks, the stabilization phase is complete. By then, your baby should be sleeping through the night on a regular basis. When we speak of *sleeping through the night*, we are referring to 7 to 8 hours of uninterrupted sleep. A *regular basis* refers to continuing that pattern for at least three consecutive days. That may occur any time between the tenth day and the eighth week, with the average PDF baby sleeping through the night by the sixth week.

NOTE: If your baby is not sleeping through the night by eight weeks, don't worry about it. Although rare, 2%-3% of PDF babies begin sleeping through the night at ten and eleven weeks. When they do, they sleep 10 to 11 hours, catching up to all the other PDF babies.

The average number of feedings in a 24-hour period will be seven before your baby is sleeping through the night and six thereafter. Although you will be dropping the nighttime feeding at this point, you will not be reducing your baby's caloric intake. Your child's nutritional needs will be met in six feedings instead of seven.

If you stick to a very strict 3-hour routine, you can fit eight feedings into a 24-hour period. There is nothing wrong with a conservative schedule if you choose to do so for the first four to six weeks. Under normal circumstances, your baby will take seven feedings in a 24-hour period.

What should you do if your baby sleeps through the night only to awaken at 5:00 a.m., while his normal routine does not start until 6:30 a.m.? You have three choices. The first choice is to wait 10 or 15 minutes to make sure he is truly awake. He may be passing through an active sleep state, moving to deeper sleep. A second possibility is to feed your baby and then put him back down. Wake him at 7:00 a.m. and feed him again. Although that is less than 3 hours, and he may not take much at that feeding, the advantage will be that your baby stays on his morning routine. A third option is to offer a feeding at 5:00 a.m., treating that as your first feeding of the day. In that case, you would adjust the rest of the baby's morning schedule so that by early afternoon he is back on his daily routine.

Initially when a baby begins to sleep through the night, a nursing mother may experience some slight discomfort for the first couple of nights. It takes a couple of days for your body to make the proper adjustments to the baby's new routine.

CONSIDERING CONTEXT

Do not be a legalistic parent. A legalistic parent is one

who elevates the method over the principle. We have all heard the cliché "Let's keep things in context." The most notable aspect of a legalist is that he or she rejects context. Responding to the context of a situation does not mean suspending the principles of PDF. Rather, you are able to focus on the right response in the short term without compromising your long-term objectives. A routine is to serve the parent, not the reverse.

There will be times when the context of a situation will dictate a temporary suspension of some of the guidelines presented. Remember, as a parent you are endowed with experience, wisdom, and common sense. Trust these attributes first, not an extreme of emotion or the rigidity of the clock. The mother that feeds her baby every time he cries is as legalistic as the parent who lets the clock rule each feeding time. When special situations arise, allow context to be your guide.

Here are some examples of context and PDF flexibility:

1. Your two-week-old baby was sleeping contentedly until his older brother decided to visit him. He is now awake and crying with another 30 minutes left before his next scheduled feeding. What should you do? You can first try settling the baby back down by patting him on the back or holding him. Placing him in his infant seat is a second option. A third option is to feed him and rework the next feed/wake/nap cycle. (Also, instruct the older brother to check with you before he visits his sleeping sibling.)

2. You are on an airplane and your baby begins to fuss— loudly. You just fed him 2 hours ago. What should you do? The answer is simple—consider others. Do not let your baby's routine get in the way of considering others. Failure to act will stress you and the rest of the

passengers. You might play with him, entertain him, or feed him. Although you normally would not offer food before 3 hours, the context of the situation dictates that you suspend your normal routine. When you arrive at your destination, get back to your basic routine. That's the balance!

3. You have been driving for 4 hours, which is your baby's normal time between feedings. Your baby is still asleep and there is another 40 minutes to travel. As a parent in control, you may choose to awaken your baby and feed him or wait until you get to your destination.

4. You just fed your baby and dropped him off at the church nursery or at the babysitter's house. You are planning to return within 1½ hours. Should you leave a bottle of breast milk or formula just in case? The answer is yes. Babysitters and nursery workers provide a valuable service to young parents. Because their care extends to other children, they should not be obligated to follow your routine exactly the way you do. If your baby fusses, you will want the caretaker to have the option of offering a bottle (even though it will have been less than 3 hours). It will not throw your child off his routine to receive an intermittent feeding sooner than 3 hours a few times during the week.

Most of your day will be fairly routine and predictable. But there will be times when you may need more flexibility due to unusual circumstances. Your life will be less tense if you consider the context of each situation and respond appropriately for the benefit of everyone. Right parental responses often determine whether their child is a blessing to others, or a source of discomfort.

SAMPLE SCHEDULE

On the next page, we have provided a sample schedule that you can personalize. Just remember the basic rule: feed every 2½ to 3 hours after the end of the last feeding, then have a waketime, followed by a naptime. The various activities listed alongside the waketimes are only suggestions. This work sheet is based on seven to eight feedings in a 24-hour period and is a guide for your first six to eight weeks.

Feeding	What to Do

Early Morning

_____ a.m.
1. Feeding - Diaper change.
2. Waketime - Rock baby and sing; place on back in crib to watch mobile.
3. Down for a nap.

Midmorning

_____ a.m.
1. Feeding - Diaper change.
2. Waketime - Take a walk, run errands, or visit neighbors.
3. Down for a nap.

Afternoon

_____ p.m.
1. Feeding - Diaper change.
2. Waketime - Bathe baby and place in infant seat near a window or somewhere with a view.
3. Down for a nap.

Midafternoon

_____ p.m.
1. Feeding - Diaper change.
2. Waketime - Play with your baby; have him by your side as you read or sew.
3. Down for a nap.

Late Afternoon

_____ p.m.   1. Feeding - Diaper change.
               2. Wake time - Family time.
               3. Down for a nap.

Evening

_____ p.m.   Feeding - Diaper change and back to bed.

               NOTE: This will be your last <u>scheduled</u> feeding of the day. Do not wake your baby from that point on. Let him wake up naturally.

Late Evening *

_____ p.m.   Feeding - Diaper change and back to bed.

               *There are three possible actions that can take place with this feeding.

               1. It may become your last feeding period until morning, <u>or</u>
               2. Your baby may skip it completely and just wake sometime in the middle of the night, <u>or</u>
               3. Your baby may initially wake for this feeding. If so, feed him.

Nighttime

_____ a.m.   Feeding - Diaper change and back to bed.

Phase Two
EXTENDED NIGHT
Weeks Nine through Thirteen

During this second phase, your baby will stretch his

nighttime sleep to 10-12 hours. Bedtime will be moved to immediately after the early-evening feeding. That change will obviously necessitate dropping the late-evening feeding. By the end of the thirteenth week, your baby should be taking four feedings a day.

Phase Three
EXTENDED DAY
Weeks Fourteen through Twenty-four

Usually between the sixteenth and twenty-fourth weeks, you will introduce your baby to solid foods. Your pediatrician will direct you in that area. By the twenty-fourth week, your baby's mealtimes should begin to line up with the rest of the family's: breakfast, lunch, and dinner, with a fourth liquid feeding at bedtime.

As you begin introducing solids to your baby's diet, please note that you are not adding more feeding periods, just additional food at breakfast, lunch, and dinner. For example, at breakfast you will give cereal, then breast- or bottle-feed. Do not offer cereal alone with a supplemental liquid feeding 2 hours later. That means you are feeding every 2 hours, which is not a healthy habit. Introducing solid foods is a topic that will be discussed in Chapter 10.

As a breast-feeding mother, try to maintain four feeding periods as long as you are nursing; any less may decrease your milk supply.

Phase Four
EXTENDED ROUTINE
Weeks Twenty-five through Fifty-two

Between the ages of six and twelve months, your baby will continue to feed on three meals a day. Each meal is supplemented by baby food, with an optional fourth liquid feeding before bed. At this age, your baby should be taking two naps averaging 1½ to 2½ hours. Continue with four nursing periods during the day. The same general rules apply to formula-fed babies (see Chapter 5, "Facts On Feeding").

SUMMARY OF FIRST-YEAR FEEDING
For easy reference the following summary of your baby's first year of feeding is provided.

Phase One: Weeks 1-8
Start with seven to eight daily feedings in the first month. The number of feedings will depend on whether you begin with a strict 3-hour routine or a flexible 3- to 3½-hour routine. By the end of this phase, you should be averaging six feedings in a 24-hour period and most likely will not have a middle-of-the-night feeding.

Phase Two: Weeks 9-13
You will transition from six feedings to four or five feedings in a 24-hour period. By week thirteen, most babies easily go to a 3½- to 4-hour routine and drop the late-evening feeding.

Phase Three: Weeks 14-24
Your baby will maintain four liquid feedings in a 24-hour period, three of which will be supplemented with baby food.

Phase Four: Weeks 25-52
The process of moving a child to three meals a day should be nearly completed by the beginning of this phase.

HOW TO DROP A FEEDING
Dropping a feeding does not mean your baby will take in

less food over a 24-hour period. Actually, the amount will gradually increase, although the frequency of feedings will decrease. As your baby begins to take more food at each feeding and his metabolism stabilizes, you will begin dropping a feeding period. The three most common feedings to be dropped are:

1. Changing from a 3-hour to a 3½-hour schedule, or from a 3½-hour to a 4-hour schedule.

   If you have to consistently wake up your baby for his daytime feedings, that is a strong indication that he can go longer between feedings. Generally, your baby will be capable of moving to a 4-hour routine by three months of age.

2. Dropping the middle-of-the-night feeding.

   Many babies drop this feeding on their own by the sixth week; one night they just sleep until morning. Some babies gradually stretch the distance between the 10 p.m. and the 6 a.m. feedings. If you hear your baby stirring or beginning to cry, wait a little bit (5-15 minutes) before going in. At this age, he is waking more because of conditioning (his biological clock) than from a need for food or comfort.

   There are some little ones whose internal clocks get stuck at the nighttime feeding. Parental guidance can help reset that clock. If you have a digital timepiece and notice that your baby is waking near to the same time each night, that is a strong indicator that his biological clock is stuck. To correct the problem, wait for a weekend when no one has to get up early for work. At least on a weekend you can sleep in if there is any noise disturbance during the night. When your baby awakens, do not rush right in. Any crying will be temporary, lasting from 5-45 minutes. Remember, it will be temporary! Some parents fear that not responding right away will make their baby feel unloved or insecure. On the contrary, it is cruel not to help your child gain the skill of sleeping through the night. Trying to manipulate this skill by taking the baby into bed with you will delay the learning process. Generally, it takes three nights to establish a new routine, one that allows for continuous sleep for both mom and baby.

3. Dropping the late-evening feeding.

This process occurs anywhere from two months on and is usually the trickiest feeding to eliminate. Having grown accustomed to sleeping all night, some parents are reluctant to drop the late-evening feeding for fear that the baby will awaken in the middle of the night starving.

Sometimes in the process of eliminating feedings, bending a guideline may be necessary. If we assume that your baby is on a 4-hour schedule (6 a.m., 10 a.m., 2 p.m., 6 p.m., and 10 p.m.) and you think he is ready to drop the last feeding, then instead of eliminating the 10 p.m. feeding completely, try backing it up 15 minutes per day until you arrive at the time you desire. For a while, your baby's last two feedings may be less than 3 hours apart, which is permissible during this transition time.

The rest of the day may change until you end up with a new 4-hour format, which will look like this: 8 a.m., 12 p.m., 4 p.m., and 8 p.m. (or whatever times suit your family).

QUESTIONS FOR REVIEW

1. List the three activities of your baby's routine.

   a.

   b.

   c.

2. From the list above, what exception applies to the late-evening and middle-of-the-night feedings?

3. How do you measure the time between feedings?

4. When should you wake a sleeping baby, and when should you let him sleep?

5. How long should a first-time mother continue with the 2½- to 3½-hour routine? Why?

6. One night your baby sleeps from 11:00 p.m. to 5:30 a.m. However, the first feeding of the day is usually at 7:00 a.m. What are three possible parenting responses?

   a.

   b.

   c.

8

WAKETIME AND NAPS

In this chapter, we will examine the last two activities in your baby's routine: waketime and naptime. One common mistake made when following a routine is to reverse the order of these last two activities—that is, putting the baby down for a nap right after his feeding. Because newborns tend to be sleepy, you will initially have to work at keeping your baby awake during his feedings and for a short period thereafter. If you switch naptime and waketime, you will be wondering why your baby cries so much.

We discourage parents from allowing their babies to fall asleep without having received a full feeding. You can avoid that by including a diaper change halfway through the feeding, by making sure your baby is not too warm (warmth enhances sleep), or by placing a cool, damp face cloth on his feet. Do not bounce or jiggle your infant in an attempt to keep him awake.

If nothing works, put him down to sleep, but do not feed him before the start of the next cycle. This is one of the only times when the clock can authoritatively guide a feeding decision. Teach your baby how and when to eat. Babies learn very quickly how to become snackers and they as easily learn how to take a complete meal. Either way, the parent guides the results.

WAKETIME
Waketime activities include times when you and your baby will be together and times when your baby will explore his new world alone. One thing is certain, your baby does not need to be entertained by you all day long.

Mom, Dad, and Baby Together

Feeding: Whether bottle or breast-feeding, you will spend much of your day holding your baby while feeding him.

Singing: From birth, a baby responds to his mom's and dad's voices. Talk and sing to your baby during wake-times, remembering that learning is always taking place.

Reading: It is never too soon to read to your baby or to show him colorful picture books (especially cardboard or plastic ones that the baby can explore more on his own). He loves to hear the sound of your voice and inflections.

Bathing: This is another pleasant routine for you and your baby. You can sing, tell him which part of his body you are washing, or just have fun splashing.

Walking: Taking time for a stroll outside is great for you and your little one. You can sing or talk while you are walking, and the fresh air is good for both of you.

Playing: Initially, you can't play much with a newborn. A few early play activities are flirting with him, smiling, talking, and gently moving his arms and legs.

Baby Alone

Pictures: Putting bright pictures and patterns around the nursery is a great way to visually stimulate your baby.

Mobiles: Moving musical mobiles help your baby learn to track with his eyes.

Gym: Crib gyms and objects that dangle over your baby and rattle when he bats at them help his hand-eye coordination. Batting is the necessary preparation for reaching out and holding objects. (For safety's sake, the crib gym should not be dangled over the baby once he learns to sit up.)

Swing: Putting a baby in a swing allows him to watch what is going on around him. Swings are especially helpful for calming fussy newborns. However, don't get into the habit of letting your baby fall asleep in a swing, since he needs to learn to fall asleep on his own.

Infant Seat: This item is another way for your baby to sit up and take notice of his world. Sometimes toys or books can be hung from an overhead handle.

Playpen: Start at one month of age with the playpen. A four-week-old baby can spend some waketime in an infant seat placed in the playpen in view of a mobile. Also, allow the child to take a nap once in a while in the playpen.

Having some of this equipment—whether new, used, or borrowed, is helpful, but it is certainly not a necessity. In addition to feeding, changing, and bathing your baby, you might have at least one playtime a day when the baby has your full attention for 15 minutes or so. Dad also needs to spend time each day with the baby, in addition to possible feeding times.

NAPTIME

Naps are not an option based on your baby's wants. When naptime comes, the baby goes down. It is that simple. For optimal development, children need daytime rest. A toddler's ability to take a nap depends on the habits he has developed in his first year. Do not underestimate the importance of your baby's nap. Naps will tend to fall in place naturally. Even when your routine changes and your baby is more wakeful, naps are still very important.

> **NOTE:** While following your feeding, wake, and sleep routine, you can plan that the last 1½ hours of your 3-hour cycle will be for a nap. When a 4-hour cycle is established, your child will sleep the last 1½ to 2 hours of that cycle.

When your baby has been up for the appropriate duration and begins to show signs of fussiness, it is time for a nap. There may be a brief period of fussing or crying when put down for his nap. Do not be deterred from doing what is best for him. Crying is not the terrible beast that some of the last generation of medical practitioners thought it was. Some crying is a normal part of a baby's day and some babies will cry a few minutes in the process of settling themselves to sleep.

Crying for 15-20 minutes is not going to hurt your baby physically or emotionally. He will not lose brain cells, experience a drop in IQ, or have feelings of rejection that will leave him manic-depressive at age thirty. You do not undo all the love and care of the waking hours with a few minutes of crying. Ironically, some of the most fussy and irritable babies we come across are those whose parents continually block all their crying by holding, rocking, or feeding them as soon as they start to fuss.

SLEEPING PATTERNS

Unlike feeding patterns, infant sleep behavior has more variation because of individual differences. Remember, stable sleep patterns are based on stable hunger patterns. When there are a number of changes in your baby's eating patterns, there will be corresponding changes in his sleep patterns.

Newborn

Newborns will sleep 16-20 hours per day, including the period of sleep between each feeding. Under PDF, this sleep will come in six to eight naps (depending on the number of daily feedings). For the first couple of weeks, your baby may be very sleepy. That will necessitate you working to keep him awake during feeding times.

Avoid letting your baby snack at meal times. Frequent snacking during the day is the enemy of nighttime sleep. If your baby falls asleep at the breast, even after your best efforts to keep him awake, then put him down for a nap. He may sleep until the next feeding, but do not allow him to sleep longer. On the other hand, if your baby starts waking too soon between feedings, then you will need to work harder to keep him awake longer before putting him down.

Two Months

If you follow the principles of PDF, this will be the month your baby drops his nighttime feeding and begins sleeping

7-8 hours continuously. Naps during the day should be at least 1½ hours. Seventy percent of PDF babies drop the middle of-the-night feeding on their own. The remaining 30% need a little nudge. This may involve some crying, which may be as short as 5 minutes or off and on as long as 1 hour. It usually takes three days to establish unbroken sleep cycles at this age.

> **NOTE:** It is not unusual for two- or three-month-old PDF babies to awaken around 5:00 or 5:30 a.m. and talk to themselves for up to an hour. Afterward, they usually go back to sleep for another hour or so. This quirky phase can go on for a week or up to a month. If you start to respond each time you hear a noise from the cradle, then 5:00 a.m. will become your baby's waketime—and yours too.

Three to Five Months

During this period, your baby will drop his late-evening feeding, leaving four feeding periods during the day. Nighttime sleep will average 10-12 hours. The baby will have three daytime naps between 1½ to 2 hours each, resulting in a longer waketime. Once the third nap is dropped, both waketime and the remaining naptimes will increase in duration.

Six to Sixteen Months

Your baby will drop his late-afternoon/early-evening nap around six months of age, leaving two naps: one in the morning and one in the afternoon. The naps are usually about 2 hours each. (For more information on this period of development, please see *BABYWISE II.*)

Sixteen Months and Older

Between sixteen and twenty months, the morning nap is dropped. Your baby should be sleeping 10-12 hours at night and 2-3 hours during one afternoon nap.

Waking Up Happy

Between four and six months, infants generally develop a wakeup disposition—one that you highly influence. Your baby's disposition can be happy and content when you follow three basic rules for naps.

Rule 1: Mom, not the baby, decides when the nap starts.

Rule 2: Mom, not the baby, decides when the nap ends.

Rule 3: If your baby wakes up crying or cranky, it is most often because he has not had sufficient sleep. Other factors to consider are a dirty diaper, a noisy neighbor, sickness coming on, or an arm or leg stuck between the crib slats.

After having been put down for a nap, your baby will move from an active sleep state to relaxed sleep in 30-45 minutes. In the next 30-45 minutes, he will move from relaxed sleep back to active sleep. At the end of that cycle, he may begin to stir and cry. Parents often interpret that to mean naptime is over. Going in to pick up the baby, they assume his crankiness is his natural way of waking up. But that is not the case.

If your baby is waking up cranky or crying, he is most likely not getting enough sleep. Even though he may cry, your baby will probably go right back to sleep in 10 minutes for another 30-40 minutes of rest. When your

baby gets enough sleep, you will notice a happy disposition. The baby will make happy cooing sounds, letting
you know it is time to get him up.

SUMMARY

When your baby starts to sleep through the night, people
will invariably say, "You're just lucky," or "You've got an
easy baby." Neither of those statements is true. Your baby
is sleeping through the night because you trained him to
do so. You can take the credit for your success. But do
keep this fact in perspective: getting your baby to sleep
through the night is not the final goal of parenting—but
we believe it does represent a right beginning.

QUESTIONS FOR REVIEW

1. What common mistake is made in relation to waketime and
   naptime?

2. In the first month, your baby may be very sleepy. What are
   some things you can do to keep him awake?

3. In relation to the previous question, if your baby does not stay awake, what should you do?

4. Are naps optional for infants? Explain.

5. When you follow a feeding, waking, and sleeping routine, how much time should be devoted for a nap in a 3-hour cycle? In a 4-hour cycle?

6. Summarize the three "wake-up-happy" rules.

a.

b.

c.

7. What is the most common reason for your baby to wake up cranky or crying?

9

WHEN YOUR BABY CRIES

Why do babies cry? Shakespeare's King Lear says, "When we are born we cry that we are come to this great stage of fools" (IV, vi, 187). When a baby cries and gnaws at his hands, we often assume he must be hungry and should be fed. There are many reasons babies cry, but it is amazing that hunger is the only reason the average person considers! Besides crying when they are hungry, babies cry when they are tired, wet, sick, bored, frustrated, out of their routine, fed too often, or simply because that is what normal, healthy babies do. As a parent, you must learn to assess your baby's cry so you can respond properly.

THE POWER OF A CRY
An infant's cry has a great influence on his development, not because of the cry itself, but because of how the parents respond. Throughout the day, your baby has definite needs for you to meet. You should not define his needs so much by the sound of his cry as by your assessment of that cry. Assessment is important.

In early infancy, crying is a noncognitive way of communicating both need and displeasure. Cries vary in purpose and intensity. The hunger cry is different from the sick cry. The sleepy cry is different from the "cuddle-me" cry. And the distress cry differs from the demanding cry. Crying varies in volume. Sometimes it will be nothing more than a gentle whimper; other times, it is a violent protest. Attempts to minimize or block all crying can very easily increase stress rather than decrease it, especially in light of the fact that emotional tears carry out of the body chemically activated stress hormones.

Those who are most affected by a baby's cry are the parents (although they do possess a greater cry tolerance than grandparents). No parent takes pleasure in hearing that sound, and neither will you. This is especially true if you are a firsttime parent, because you have never experienced as powerful an emotion as the one caused by your baby's cry. It is a sound that can cause you to wonder if you have done something wrong. You will feel that way not because crying itself is bad, but because you will be unfamiliar with the emotions of uncertainty that crying evokes.

TEACHING YOUR BABY TO LOVE?

Does responding immediately, on cue, with breast-feeding to a baby's every cry teach him how to love? Does not responding to every cry on cue with breast-feeding teach disappointment? We believe that kind of thinking reduces love and security to a process rather than a relationship.

There is no evidence to prove that an immediate response to every cry teaches a baby anything about love, just as there is no evidence to prove that a little crying fosters feelings of insecurity. A child learns love and gains security from the total context of the parent-child relationship, not from any one particular action.

Experience teaches that parents who desire to demonstrate true love to their children will put aside their own emotions for the sake of the child. They will tolerate a little crying if by their assessment it is the best plan of action for the baby, such as when a baby might need to settle in for a nap or his night's sleep.

THE INEVITABLE CONFLICT
Conflict originates in philosophy. Does crying create within a baby irreversible latent effects on personality development in later years, as suggested by attachment theorist? Should we equate human offspring with animal offspring as Darwin suggests? We think not. The question is not whether crying is bad for your baby, but whether blocking _all_ crying is good for him. We believe the answer is no! By persisting with a "block-that-cry" attitude, a mother loses confidence in her own ability to make decisions later. Furthermore, there is not a great amount of difference between blocking a baby's cry and offering food at each whimper or wearing him in a sling all day so he won't cry.

A mom who picks up her baby and offers the breast each time he cries is teaching him that food is his source of comfort, not Mom. That explains why Nathan is not easily comforted by secondary caregivers. It may also explain the obesity problem with our nation's youth and why more and more adults are turning to food as a method of stress relief. They have been trained that way from the beginning. Here we are not equating a fat baby and a fat adolescent. But feeding problems in infancy, such as overfeeding or disregarding healthy eating patterns, may result in eventual obesity.

There is another consideration. What will happen to Nathan, whose parents have conditioned him to expect immediate gratification, when it is no longer possible to satisfy him immediately? What happens when the second or third child enters the family? Think of the emotional trauma he will experience. This painful experience is described by mothers as "the baby becoming unglued." The child is so conditioned to immediate response that he cannot cope with a delayed response. Now the child is emotionally fragile rather than emotionally stable.

Nathan's mom has been bombarded by clichés such as "You can't hurt a baby by picking him up whenever he cries. After all, you can't spoil him by loving him too much." Of course you can hurt a baby by picking him up too much. Ryan's mother is more discerning. She realizes that the result is not a spoiled child but a predisposition for immediate gratification that becomes a destructive influence on his pretoddler and toddler development. Immediate gratification training negatively impacts learning structures that enhance the skills of sitting, focusing, and concentrating. Right learning structures lead to right learning patterns.

Babies not only become conditioned to being picked up at a whimper but also become abnormally dependent on it. How sad to think that Nathan's parents are unknowingly training him to use crying as his only mode of expression.

THE PDF BABY
It is commonly observed that babies under the PDF plan tend to cry less in the long run than babies who are demand-fed. The reason? Infants put on a routine become confident and secure in that routine. Their lives have order and they learn the lesson of flexibility early in life.

Babies who settle into regular and predictable rhythms of activity develop greater tolerance to frustration and learn to use modes of communication other than crying. Ryan expresses himself with happy sounds, such as cooing, and by excited body motions, such as bouncing. These are additional modes of baby talk.

CRIES TO LISTEN FOR

Some crying will be normal and expected, but there are other identifiable cries you will want to check.[9] A high-pitched and piercing cry may be a signal of either internal or external body injury. That type of cry, if persistent, should be brought to the attention of your pediatrician.

A marked change in your baby's crying pattern, such as a sudden increase in the frequency and the duration of crying, or a weak, mousy cry, may be a warning of illness. Be sure to discuss this with your pediatrician. Cries indicating hunger or thirst are predictable with PDF babies. With demand-fed babies, their cries are unpredictable, leaving Mom and Dad guessing and anxious.

You can be sure that what you hear is not a hunger-and-thirst cry if your baby is satisfied after a feeding. Babies who cry routinely and act hungry after 2 hours are probably not getting enough food. If you are breast-feeding, check your milk supply and the factors which influence it. (See "Testing Your Milk Supply" in Chapter 6.)

If your baby cries routinely within 30 minutes of his feeding, it may be caused by one of several factors.

1. Trapped gas. Young babies often swallow air during feedings, which must be brought up. Burp your baby by holding him against your shoulder, on your lap, or over your knee.

2. Your diet. Consider what you are eating if you are breast-feeding. Be careful of too many dairy products or spicy foods. You do not have to completely eliminate them, but you may have to cut back considerably.

3. <u>Fatigue</u>. Your baby is tired and needs sleep.

WHAT SHOULD I DO WHEN MY BABY CRIES?
It should go without saying that ignoring a hungry baby's cry is unacceptable. If your baby seems to be hungry all the time, the problem is not with routines in general, but with *your* routine. You may have reversed the order of waketime and naptime activities, or you may not be milk sufficient.

The latter could be caused by a number of different factors, including stress, a lack of sleep, an improper diet, a meddling mother or mother-in-law, or friends who insist you nurse their way. Abandoning your PDF routine and dropping the times of your feedings below 2½ to 3 hours has very few advantages, if any at all.

In relation to a baby's cry, the distinction between feeding philosophies is basic. Ryan's mom understands the wisdom of first assessing her baby's cry and then acting. She listens, she thinks, and then acts on her assessment.

Nathan's mom unfortunately does not take time to assess. In fact, she was told not to think, just react according to her feelings. But feelings are not the basis for sound decision making. To deny the importance of careful assessment is to deny the parents their leadership role. Leaders must be clear headed, ready to make decisions. They are not to be driven by their passions. Practically, emotional mothering can set the stage for child abuse. It creates a vicious cycle. A predominant characteristic of abusive parents is the thoughtless responses directed toward innocent children. Too often those responses are fueled by sleepless nights and a child trained to be demanding.

How should you respond when your baby cries? Unless you sense your baby is in danger, take a moment to listen and assess his crying. After a brief assessment, take the appropriate action. Here are some practical steps to follow.

<u>Listen</u> for the type of cry. Even in the early days and weeks, you will begin to distinguish different tones and patterns in your baby's cry. By simply stopping to listen, you may find the crying ends as quickly as it began. Why listen? If a child has a dirty diaper, are you going to feed him? If your baby has trapped gas, is the answer food? If he cries because of an ear infection, is nursing the medicine?

<u>Think</u> about where your baby is in his routine. Is naptime over? Is he in the middle of his nap and in need of resettling himself? Does he need to go down for a nap? Has he been in the swing too long? Did he lose his toy? Did he spit up? Is it his fussy time? That is only a small list of why your baby might be crying. There are many reasons other than hunger for infant tears.

<u>Take action</u> based on what you have heard and reasonably concluded. Just remember, sometimes the best action to take is no action. For example, if your baby is clean, fed, and ready for naptime, let him learn how to fall asleep on his own if that is what he needs. If you try to nurse him to sleep, you have only succeeded in manipulating his sleep.

Take note of how long your baby cries. It can be comforting later to realize that all that noise (which seemed interminable at the time) really lasted only 5, 10, or 15 minutes. If you have listened, waited, and determined that the crying is not subsiding, gather more information by checking on the baby. Peek into his crib and see if he has jammed himself into a corner, in which case you would simply move him and offer a gentle pat on the back before leaving the room.

There will be times when your assessment calls for picking up your baby and holding him to reassure him everything is all right. Some special time in Mommy's arms may be all that is needed. Your assessment may produce many options, but blocking your child's cry because you can't handle it is not one of them.

WHEN DO I HOLD AND COMFORT MY BABY?

You will, of course, hold your baby many hours a day as you go through the normal process of caring and feeding. Flirt, rock, and sing when he is happy and not so happy, but do not feel you must constantly hold him during every fussy time.

Parents should comfort their baby when comfort is needed. The standard question every parent should ask is: What type of comfort should be given? A diaper change will comfort a wet baby, feeding will comfort a hungry baby, holding will comfort a startled baby, and sleep will comfort a tired baby. A baby can receive comfort in many ways and from different people. Certainly Dad, older siblings, Grandma, and Grandpa can be sources of comfort. A baby can be comforted by being held, rocked, sung to, taken for a stroller ride, or placed near music. The good news is that a mother's breasts are not the only source of comfort.

Wisdom dictates that a mother should recognize that a baby responds to different forms of comfort at different times. If you use one source exclusively, such as nursing, you are just stopping the cry and not necessarily comforting your baby.

SUMMARY

As a parent, you will learn to recognize your baby's different cries and will know how to respond with confidence. The wise parent will listen, think, and then take action. If your baby is fed, clean, dry, and healthy, but begins to cry before falling asleep, consider it just one more phase of your child's normal development.

QUESTIONS FOR REVIEW

1. Throughout the day your baby will have definite needs for you to meet. What are the right and wrong ways to define those needs?

2. What are parents teaching an infant when they pick him up and offer him food each time he cries? What problems can result from this practice?

3. What is wrong with the advice "When your baby cries, don't think, just react"?

4. If your baby cries after a feeding, what factors should you consider?

5. What three things should you do when your baby cries?

   a.

   b.

   c.

6. As it relates to comforting a baby, what is the standard question every parent should ask? Give examples.

10

THE TOPIC POOL

Here is an alphabetical listing of topics of common interest to new parents. Many of these topics are dealt with more extensively in our next series, *BABYWISE II*.

ACHIEVEMENT LEVELS

A substantial amount has been written regarding what an infant is supposed to be doing physically during the first year of life. That includes such tasks as shaking a rattle, saying "da-da," reaching for bright objects, and crawling. There are three facts to remember. *First*, a baby's basic routine enhances learning. Order is a mutual ally of cognation. *Second*, infants will differ in the age at which they master skills. There is no cause for alarm or need to compare your child with your neighbor's child. *Third*, along with his physical development, your baby will become more and more responsive to moral training. Be careful not to focus solely on your baby's physical accomplishments without giving due consideration to his developing attitudes.

BABY BLUES

Postpartum depression is commonly referred to as "baby blues" and is now receiving significant attention from the media. Physically, there is a hormonal change that takes place right after delivery. For some women, it may take longer for those hormones to be brought back into balance.

Although some women find themselves depressed and weepy several days after giving birth, not all women experience postpartum depression. Many who do have certain traits in common—they're not on a routine, they nurse frequently, and they are up several times during the night—all of which leaves them in a perpetual state of exhaustion. Each of these symptoms can be traced back to the strain that the lack of routine puts on a mother. You can greatly minimize the symptoms of postpartum depression by keeping yourself on a good routine, getting plenty of rest, and watching your diet. If you find that after several weeks you are still abnormally melancholy, talk to your obstetrician.

BABY EQUIPMENT

One thing to remember about baby equipment is that much of it is optional (a car seat is not). You do not need to follow all the recommended baby equipment lists that appear in parent magazines or in baby stores. Your baby is not going to know or care if he has coordinating furniture, so don't worry if it is not in your budget. There are some items beyond the usual high chair, stroller, changing table, and crib that would be helpful, and often you can borrow them or purchase them at a garage sale.

Baby Monitor

The monitor can serve a useful purpose by allowing you

to hear your baby if you happen to have a large home or are working outdoors during your baby's nap. There is no need to keep it by your bedside at night. You will hear your baby cry during those hours. During the still of the night, the monitor magnifies every sound your baby makes, robbing you of needed sleep. The last thing your child needs in the morning is a cranky parent.

Car Seat

A car seat should be functional, not only for your infant but also for your toddler. Think long term when you make that investment. Some car seats are very stylish and work fine for your infant, but may not be practical for a growing toddler, thus necessitating the purchase of a second car seat. An infant younger than six months does not have strong neck muscles, so please try to prevent his head from rolling from side to side while driving. This can be accomplished by rolling a diaper and putting it to the side of your baby's head.

Crib

Cribs, cradles, and cots are not products of the industrial revolution. They were household pieces of furniture used by parents throughout antiquity. Three ancient Mediterranean societies (Greek, Roman, and Hebrew) all used cribs.

The cradle, which is an infant crib with rocking motion, gained popularity in the Middle Ages. Eventually it became a status symbol of wealth. Cribs and cradles were not limited to Europe or the Mediterranean basin. Mothers in primitive settings hang cribs from the ceiling of their huts, where they can gently rock their babies as they pass by. For twentieth-century parents, the crib is one of the most basic pieces of baby furniture they will own. Give thought to the one you buy or borrow. After all, nearly half of your child's time for the first eighteen months will be spent in it.

When deciding on a crib to use, look for certain features. The mattress should fit snugly on all four sides and should be a firm mattress of good quality. A snug fit prevents the baby from getting any of his body parts stuck between the mattress and the slats. The guardrail should be at least twenty-six inches from the top of the mattress. This will discourage any attempt to climb out when he is older. The spaces between the crib slats should be no more than two and three-eighths inches apart. A crib bumper-guard is a good investment and is safer for the baby than using pillows or stuffed animals. The latter should be kept out of the newborn's crib because of the potential danger of suffocation.

The location of the crib in the room is another consideration. Avoid placing the crib near drafty windows, heat radiators, or hot air ducts. A steady blast of hot air can dry out your baby's nose and throat, leading to respiratory problems.

Infant Seat

You will use the infant seat from day one and use it more than any other piece of equipment in the early weeks and months. When your child is old enough to be spoon fed, an infant seat is preferable to a high chair, since at this age the child does not have the strength to sit up. The infant seat is not a car seat.

Infant Sling

In some third-world nations, mothers carry their babies in

decision may be made either prior to your due date because of a known condition or because of an unexpected complication during labor. In either case, competent doctors have your best interests in mind.

More unnecessary c-sections are performed today than in yesteryears. There are two primary reasons for that fact. First, we have greater technology to save babies. Second, there are more lawsuits against obstetricians and gynecologists, forcing them to exercise conservative treatment. Keep in mind that a c-section is a medical decision that in no way reflects on your motherhood. There is no need to feel guilty or embarrassed over it. Just be thankful that you and your baby are healthy.

CHURCH NURSERIES AND BABYSITTERS

Nursery workers and babysitters provide a wonderful service. Unfortunately, some moms and dads demand that the nursery workers keep their babies on a rigid routine. We believe in gracious deference and an appreciative attitude when leaving your child in the nursery or in other special babysitting situations. Nursery workers are not obligated to maintain your baby's schedule, because there is no way they can keep track of ten, fifteen, or twenty different schedules.

When your baby goes to the nursery, leave a bottle of water, formula, or breast milk and give the nursery worker the freedom to do what he or she thinks is best. It will not disrupt your baby's routine to be fed sooner than what you would normally plan. You will be able to get your baby back on routine later that day.

We are encouraged by the fact that so many parents understand the value of order in their lives and their children's lives. But sometimes people redefine order to mean rigidity, and that leads to imbalance. Balance includes the right proportions of structure and flexibility.

CIRCUMCISION

Circumcision is almost as old as history itself. The practice was historically (though not exclusively) a Jewish rite. Today medical experts and studies tend to agree on the value of circumcision, although not all agree on the necessity of it. Evidence suggests that circumcision may decrease the risk of urinary tract infection and that it virtually eliminates the possibility of cancer of the penis. Parents should also consider the social ramifications of circumcision. How will your son feel in a locker room in his school years?

For the infant, circumcision is not the traumatic experience that some portray. His minor surgery and any discomfort felt will not be rooted in his memory any more than being given the heel stick for his PKU test soon after delivery.

CRIB DEATH

The unexpected death of a seemingly healthy baby is referred to as Sudden Infant Death Syndrome (SIDS) or crib death. What do we know about this syndrome? It is responsible for 7,000 deaths a year and is neither predictable nor preventable. There are more male victims, especially among those who are born prematurely, and there is a higher incidence rate among babies of minorities, young single mothers, and those who smoke.

A child can be victimized by SIDS anytime during the first year, with the highest percentage of incidents occurring between the second and fourth months. More babies die of SIDS in the winter months than in summer and more in colder climates than in warmer ones.

Some family bed advocates suggest there is a correlation between SIDS and infants sleeping with their parents. It is suggested that sleeping with your baby can decrease the possibility of SIDS. The conclusion is drawn from comparative data compiled in third-world nations where fewer SIDS cases were reported among children who slept with their parents compared to SIDS cases in North America. The conclusion begs for clarification. Most third-world nations are found in warmer climates, which means SIDS will be 4-5 times less due to the absence of cold weather. Also, when a comparison is made within the same society, families that sleep with their children have equal or higher rates of infant deaths than those who do not sleep with their children.

Some researchers suggest that putting a baby on his back for sleep rather than on his tummy will reduce the chance of crib death. That research is not conclusive, and the method of gathering supportive data is questionable. To state that babies in Nigeria have a lower SIDS rate than American babies because they're put down on their backs is entirely too simplistic, with many variables left unaccounted for. We suggest you speak to your health care provider about any questions concerning SIDS and the positioning of your baby. Rare as it may be, parents should be concerned with the possibility that their baby could aspirate from an abnormally high amount of vomit that has no place to go if he is placed on his back. At least when on his tummy or side, gravity will not allow any vomit to return to his system.

One last word about crib death. The one thing that most pediatricians agree upon is the need for a firm mattress of good quality. Soft mattresses with questionable stuffing material should be avoided. Spend the extra money to get a good mattress.

DIAPERS

As new parents, you have a choice between disposable or cloth diapers. It really is a matter of personal preference. As a general rule, you will change your baby's diaper at each feeding. For demand-fed babies, that could be as many as 12 times a day. PDF babies average six to seven diaper changes a day, coinciding with their feedings.

At the nighttime feeding it is not necessary to change your baby's diaper with the exception of one that is soaked or soiled. Remember, your goal is for your baby to sleep through the night, not to wake up for a diaper change. When your baby begins to sleep through the night, use a medium diaper. They will seem larger only because today's babies are not expected to sleep through the night as early as those on PDF.

DIAPER RASH

A diaper rash may be caused by yeast infections, food allergies, new teeth, or sitting too long in a messy diaper. If your baby has sensitive skin, he may be more prone to diaper rash. Have your pediatrician recommend an over-the-counter medication for minor irritations or a prescription medication for more severe problems.

FUSSY TIME OR COLIC?

A fussy time in the late afternoon is not uncommon. That is true with both bottle- and breast-fed infants and should be expected. There is no reason for you to be anxious, because you are in good company. Literally millions of mothers and fathers are going through the same thing at just about the same time each day.

For most babies, having a fussy time is a way of releasing body energy. If the child is not comforted by the baby swing, an infant seat, siblings, or Grandma, consider the crib. At least there he has the chance of falling asleep.

If you have a baby who becomes exceptionally and continuously fussy, consider the possibility that he is hungry. How is your milk supply? Are you eating right? Go back to Chapter 5 and look at the factors influencing your milk production. Also check what you're eating. Hot, spicy foods as well as a large intake of dairy products are common contributors to fussy behavior at all times of the day. Adding the wrong foods to your diet can amplify the normal fussy time and create nightmares for young parents. Because Nathan is not on a routine, he is much more likely to be a fussy baby. Ryan, on the other hand, may have a fussy time, but will not be characterized as a 24-hour fussy baby.

Do not misinterpret your child's fussy time as colic. Colic is very rare in PDF babies but is intensified in demand-fed babies. The last thing you want to put into an irritated stomach is food, but that is usually the first thing many mothers do. The baby cries, and they offer the breast. The baby nurses because of reflex, not because he finds comfort in more food.

Very few infants truly suffer from colic. It appears as early as the second week and usually disappears at the end of the twelfth week. The spells usually occur in the early evening, at night, and right after feeding. The baby may draw up his legs and clench his fists as if he is in pain. He may act hungry but begin crying part way through the feeding.

Contact your pediatrician if these symptoms occur. Having a child that cries for hours for no apparent reason can be very frustrating and emotionally draining on you as parents. If your baby does suffer from colic, the best thing you can do for him is to keep him on a routine that will allow his stomach to rest between feedings.

GRANDPARENTS
There is a special relationship between the third generation and the first. Take advantage of every opportunity for a grandparent to enjoy your child, but keep it within reason. Do not assume your parents want to babysit or

abuse their generous offer to do so. Do not surrender your parenting responsibilities to your parents. While they may very much enjoy their grandchildren, they are not the parents—you are.

Many grandparents travel a great distance to visit soon after the baby is born. That visit can be either a blessing or a problem, depending on your relationship and just how like-minded you are. You may want to ask the traveling grandparents to visit ten days to two weeks after the baby is born. By then you will have worked through your basic parenting approach and will feel somewhat comfortable with what you are doing. Having a high-powered, take-charge relative come in right after birth can be very hard on a new mother's emotions. A husband can help by protecting his wife from unwelcome intrusions.

GROWTH SPURTS

Growth spurts for your infant will probably begin around four to six weeks of age. If you are breast-feeding, these spurts may necessitate an extra feeding for a couple of days to increase your milk supply for your baby's increased demand. If you are feeding approximately every 4 hours when this happens, drop back to 3 hours a couple of times a day. If you are bottle-feeding and suspect your baby is experiencing a growth spurt, simply offer more formula per feeding. However, beware of using growth spurts as an excuse for prolonged "extra" feedings.

IMMUNIZATION

The ability to protect our children from the tragedies of polio, smallpox, and other deadly diseases is one of the advantages of our day. Medical research has provided us with effective immunizations that build up antibodies to fight off invading diseases. But the vaccines are useless if the child never receives them. Although the legitimacy of some vaccines is in question, parents are responsible to see that their child is fully protected.

The eight common vaccinations offered are polio, diphtheria, pertussis (whooping cough), tetanus, rubella (German measles), mumps, measles, and *Hemophilus influenza*, type b. Most pediatricians start routine immunizations when a baby is two months old.

Immunization Schedule

DPT	2-4- 6-18 months and 4-6 years
Polio	2-4-18 months and 4-6 years
Hib	2-4- 6-15 months
TB Test	12 months
Measles	15 months
Mumps	15 months
Rubella	15 months
Tetanus	14-16 years
Diphtheria	14-16 years

Immunization schedules change frequently as better vaccines and more information become available. Ask your pediatrician to give you a current vaccination schedule.

JAUNDICE IN NEWBORNS

Newborn jaundice is a condition, not a disease. It is characterized by a yellow tinge to the skin and eyes caused by the pigment bilirubin in the blood. A mild degree of jaundice is common in most newborns. If it appears to be more serious after the second day, frequent blood tests are done and conservative treatment initiated.

Part of that treatment includes an increase in fluid intake. You do not necessarily have to nurse more often. Sticking with a strict 2½-hour feeding routine is normally sufficient to bring down the bilirubin levels. There may be other liquid substitutes recommended by your pediatrician. Babies with moderately raised levels of bilirubin are also treated with special fluorescent lights that help to break down the yellow pigment. Your doctor will determine the program of treatment that is right for your baby. Because a newborn with jaundice will tend to sleep more, make sure you wake your baby and feed him at least every 3 hours. Jaundice is usually easily controlled, but it could develop into a dangerous situation when ignored or left untreated.

THE MICROWAVE AND THE BOTTLE

Occasionally you may want to heat your baby's bottle in a microwave oven. That can be dangerous if certain precautions are not taken. Microwaves heat foods unevenly, so be sure to shake the bottle well after heating and squirt a dab of milk on your wrist to test for warmth. Breast milk, unlike formula, can be destroyed in the heating process if care is not taken. When heating your baby's bottle, be sure to loosen the top to allow for heat expansion, or it may explode.

NURSING TWINS

For a mother to nurse twins successfully, the parent-directed feeding plan is a must. Assign one breast to each twin and keep them on that breast for all feedings. That will allow the supply to keep up with the unique demand of each twin. Let one set the pace and keep them both on that schedule. If that means you must wake one, do it. If this means one must cry before his feeding, let him.

Right after they are born, you can nurse them simultaneously using a football hold—arms bent to support the back of each baby while each head rests on a breast. As they grow, you will have to nurse one at a time. Beyond that distinction, you will be able to implement all the other aspects of the parent-directed feeding plan, including feeding routines and sleeping through the night. May you thoroughly enjoy your "double portion"!

PACIFIERS/THUMBSUCKING

Breast-feeding mothers should not let themselves be used as pacifiers. Some infants have a need to suck a little longer after feeding time. An actual pacifier is very useful for them. That is especially true of infants who nurse so efficiently that feeding time lasts a total of only 5 to 10 minutes. Pacifiers can also be used to extend the time between feedings when a baby is fussy but not hungry. However, be careful not to use the pacifier as a plug whenever your baby fusses. Do not create habits that will have to be broken later.

Some children will not take a pacifier but find their thumbs. That is fine. Consider how long you will use the pacifier or allow your child to suck his thumb. If thumb-sucking persists past two years, limit it to the child's bedroom. That boundary will help you eliminate the practice later on.

SLEEPING WITH YOUR BABY

It is common for children in third-world countries to sleep in the same bed with their parents. In most cases this is done for pragmatic reasons: There is only one bed and often only one room. Poverty forces the sleeping arrangements, not the pursuit of psychological health. For modern America, the family bed finds its roots in the birth trauma theory. As stated previously, the practice allows for the constant presence of the mother required by the hypothesis.

The family bed is unsafe. The Consumer Protection Safety Commission warns parents against sleeping with their infants because of the death hazard. They are joined by the vast majority of health care professionals in America who also discourage the practice. The child could smother underneath a sleeping adult, become wedged between the mattress or a nearby wall, or suffocate face down, especially on a waterbed. These terrible things do happen. There is not a single benefit gained that can possibly outweigh the risk.

Some countries discourage the practice altogether. New Zealand, for example, has cut down on infant death dramatically by educating young parents to the dangers of such a practice. As more infant deaths are reported in America, state legislators are beginning to consider laws to discourage the practice. Why take a chance like that?

Sleeping with your baby creates needs but does not fulfill them. Your child will not be any more secure, feel more loved, or have any greater advantage in life than a child who sleeps alone. What the nighttime parenting advocates gloss over are the sleep problems created as the child grows older. We believe it hinders the development of trust between parent and child, since the child is never given the opportunity to learn how to trust. The child who can sleep by himself, knowing that Mom and Dad will come when needed, is much more secure than the child who is never by himself and cannot exist outside his parents' presence. With the latter, trust is based upon proximity rather than a relationship. The measure of a child's security is never found in the presence of his parent, but in how well the child copes away from his parent. The benefits of shared sleep are clearly over-exaggerated.

Shared sleep confuses infant sleep cycles. Separation anxiety is another concern when the child is asked to leave Mom and Dad's bed. If an infant is placed in his own bed and in his own room right from the beginning, no separation anxiety takes place, since no dependent nighttime relationship was established. Shared sleep has proven problematic for many nursing mothers, since the fear of rolling on top of the baby creates anxiety, thus affecting sleep and milk production.

Contrast the nighttime peace associated with a baby sleeping soundly in his crib, to the squeezed, squirming, and disrupted sleep moms and dads who share a bed with their baby experience. As one mother states, "It wasn't as natural as they said it would be. Every sound, move, and restless fit the child made was amplified. We held our breath hoping upon hope that the child would not wake and demand of me. My comfort during the day and night became a reluctant duty and not a true expression of a mother's love. The theory robbed me of the joy of motherhood."

There is nothing wrong with a child taking a nap with Mom or Dad once in a while or with cuddling the baby in bed before everyone gets up. But patterns you establish in the first couple of days, weeks, and months, whether right or wrong, will become those to which your little one will adjust. The longer wrong patterns persist, the harder they will be to break.

SPITTING UP

This is a common event in the life of every infant. At first it may be frightening to a new parent, but it is normal and not a cause for alarm. Proper burping during and after feeding can minimize and sometimes eliminate that problem. Your baby may have taken in more milk than he needed. Refeeding is not usually necessary. Keep in mind that babies vary tremendously; some rarely spit up, while others spit up all the time. If your child is growing, gaining weight, and is happy and healthy, then he is fine.

Projectile vomiting is not the same thing as spitting up. Instead of returning just part of his meal, the baby powerfully ejects the entire contents of his stomach. If this type of vomiting happens routinely, call your pediatrician.

STARTING SOLIDS

Parent-directed feeding continues with the addition of solids (baby and table foods) to your baby's menu. Add solids at existing family mealtimes, working toward three meals a day. With the production of saliva at about three months, you will see the baby preparing for a change in his menu (although you will not begin solids until he is four to six months of age).

In your child's first year, the calories he gains from liquids (breast milk or formula) are of primary importance. During the second half of the first year, a gradual transition occurs. Though your baby may still drink as much at twelve months as he did at six months, he will need more and more calories from solids.

Generally, you should start adding solids to your baby's diet between four and six months, depending on the baby's weight gain and sleep patterns. Your pediatrician will advise you. The first food to add to your baby's meals is rice cereal. Later, you will add other single-grain cereals. The exact how-to specifics of adding solids are discussed in *BABYWISE II*.

TEETHING

When a tooth begins to break through the gum, a baby experiences the condition commonly referred to as teething. Like jaundice, teething is not a disease; it's a condition of growth. Your baby's first teeth will push through between six and eight months of age. By six months, one baby out of three has one tooth, and by nine months, the average baby has three teeth. The natural process of teething should not interfere with breast-feeding, since the sucking is done by the tongue and palate, not by the gums.

Irritability, fussiness, increased salivation, and a slightly raised temperature sometimes accompany new teeth. As uncomfortable as these symptoms may be, teething is not a catch-all excuse for chronic poor behavior or a drastic change in your baby's routine.

WEANING YOUR BABY

Weaning, by today's definition, is the process by which parents offer food supplements in place of, or in addition to, mother's milk. That process begins the moment parents offer a bottle of formula or when their baby first tastes cereal. From that moment on, weaning is generally a gradual process.

From the Breast

The duration of breast-feeding has varied from the extremes of birth to fifteen years. No one can say for sure what age is ideal. For some it may be six months, for others a year. Breast-feeding for more than a year is a matter of preference, since adequate supplementary food is usually available. Several thousands of years ago, weaning took place between eighteen and twenty-four months. Three years was very rare.

At birth, infants are totally dependent on their caregiver to meet their physical needs. But they must gradually become more independent, taking small steps at a time. One such step for your baby is the ability to feed himself. You can start this process by eliminating one feeding at a time, going three to four days before dropping the next one. That time frame allows your body to make the proper adjustments in milk reduction.

Usually the late-afternoon feeding is the easiest one to drop, since it is a busy time of day. Replace each feeding with 6-8 ounces of formula or milk (depending on the child's age). Pediatricians generally recommend that parents not give their babies cow's milk until they are at least one year of age. If your baby is nine months or older, consider going straight to a cup rather than to a bottle. The transition will be easiest if you have introduced the cup prior to the weaning.

From the Bottle

When your baby is one year of age, you can begin to wean him from the bottle. Some mothers wean straight to a cup with great success. Although an infant can become very attached to his bottle, you can minimize that problem by not letting him hold it for extended periods of time. There is a difference between playing with the bottle and drinking from it. The weaning process takes time, so be prepared to be patient. Begin by eliminating the bottle at one meal, then at another, and so on.

11

NEWBORN SCENARIOS

1. Your baby has been brought to you for his very first feeding. How long will you let him nurse?

   Begin with 3 minutes per side, increasing gradually to a maximum of 15 minutes per side. (See Chapter 5.)

2. This is your first day home from the hospital. Your baby likes to sleep from 10 a.m. until 3 p.m. and eat every 3 hours the rest of the day and night. Is this routine acceptable?

   No. Your baby has his nights and days mixed up. Parent-directed feeding offers a proactive management plan for your baby. Wake your baby and feed him at 3-hour intervals during the day. In a few days, he will get his days and nights lined up with the rest of the family.

3. Your 2 week old nurses on one side, then falls asleep. Two hours later, he wants to eat again. What should you do?

You must keep your baby awake during feeding time and teach him to nurse from both sides equally. Try changing his diaper between sides, undressing him, and rubbing his head, feet, or nose. Do what you must to keep him awake and finish the task at hand which is eating. Babies learn very quickly from the laws of natural consequences. If he does not eat at one feeding, then make him wait until the next one. That will probably only happen once. Do not feed him between routine mealtimes; otherwise, you are teaching him to snack, not eat.

4. **Your baby starts to cry 2 hours after the previous feeding and seems to be hungry. You have tried to stretch it to 2 hours, but cannot get him to go longer. What is the problem?**

The most common reason a baby fails to make the 2½ hour minimum (especially babies under two weeks of age) is that the order of daytime activities has been reversed. The events must follow in this order: feeding time, waketime, then naptime. When a baby goes only 2 hours between feedings, it is usually due to the reversal of the last two activities. After the feeding time, try to keep the baby awake so that the last 1½ of a 3-hour cycle is the naptime. Check your milk supply. As we stated in Chapter 7, if your baby is hungry, feed him. But investigate why he is not reaching the minimum mark and start working toward it.

5. **You have just fed, changed, and played with your new baby. Five minutes after you put him down, he starts crying very hard, which is unusual for him. What should you do?**

Go in and check on your baby. The fact that this is not routine behavior calls for your attention. He may have a messy diaper or need to be burped. Keep in mind that since it is naptime, some crying is not unusual. Napping is a skill that needs to be learned. Don't believe the old wives' tales that your baby is signaling a need to be picked up and rocked every time he cries.

6. **How much time is appropriate for holding your baby?**

Parents should be more concerned with what is an inappropriate amount of time to hold their baby whether too little or too much. The latter is often the case with demand feeding.

If you follow the parent-directed feeding plan, you will hold your baby the appropriate amount of time during the day without sacrificing your other areas of responsibility. The fact is, you hold your baby many times throughout the day during feeding, playing, loving, and changing times. Because you are following PDF, Dad and other family members will also be holding and loving the baby.

7. **You have just fed your baby and then he spits up what looks to be a good amount of the feeding. When will you feed him again?**

Even though your baby may seem to have lost his whole meal, normally you will not feed him again until his next routine feeding. The amount of partially digested milk often can appear to be greater than it actually is. Overfeeding and doing a poor job of burping your baby are common causes for projectile vomiting. However, if this problem continues routinely, it may signal a digestive problem. For your own peace of mind and possibly for your baby's health, contact your pediatrician.

8. **Your baby is eight weeks old and has not yet slept through the night. What should you do to eliminate the middle-of-the-night feeding?**

Go back and review the specific guidelines listed in Chapter 5. Are you following them? If so, your eight-week-old baby is ready to sleep through the night for his sake and yours. If he is waking every night at basically the same time, then he is waking out of nighttime habit and not out of need. If that is the case, you may need to help him eliminate the feeding period by not physically attending to him. Normally it takes three nights of some crying before the habit is broken. He will never remember those three nights, nor will they have any negative effects on your baby. Helping him to learn nighttime sleep behavior will have positive effects and is healthier for both him and you.

9. **Your three month old has been sleeping through the night for several weeks. But now he is starting to wake up during the night. What is the problem and what should you do?**

This is not an uncommon event. Your baby is probably going through a growth spurt. For the next couple of days, add a feeding or two to your routine. If he is on a 3½ to 4-hour schedule, go back to 3 hours between feedings for a portion of your routine. This situation is temporary and will most likely be repeated in six months. It is also a prelude to your child's need for additional nutrition. Check with your pediatrician as to when your baby will start on cereal.

10. **You are at a family gathering and have just put the most popular guest (your baby) down for a nap. He begins to cry and everyone is waiting to see what you are going to do. Aunt Martha volunteers to get the baby. What should you do and say?**

Flexibility needs to be part of your plan. How old is the baby? How badly does he need to go down right now? Be sensitive to the feelings of others. If you are characterized by following a schedule, allowing Aunt Martha to get the baby this one time will not hurt your baby's routine.

11. **Your two month old has been sleeping through the night for five weeks, but last night he woke up at 3 a.m. What should you do?**

Since your baby has proven capable of sleeping through the night, we can rule out poor sleep behavior training. Assess the situation. Is your baby too warm? Does he have a cold? Did the cat jump in the crib? Use good judgment when deciding what you are going to do. However, do not create wrong sleep patterns that will only need correcting three days later.

12

PRINCIPLES FOR STARTING LATE

Unfortunately, not all parents start with the advantage of *BABYWISE*. Many awaken to the need after their babies are six, twelve, or eighteen months old and are not sleeping through the night. Is it too late for these parents? Absolutely not. If you are in that situation and desire to correct the problem, the change must begin with you.

Below are both general rules and guidelines that will help your baby establish continuous nighttime sleep.

GENERAL RULES

1. Make sure you read and understand the entire contents of *BABYWISE* before proceeding any further.

2. Do not try to make any changes while out-of-town guests or relatives are visiting. You do not need the added pressure of explaining everything you are doing.

3. Start the process of change when your baby is healthy.

GENERAL GUIDELINES

1. For the first four to five days, work on your baby's daytime routine. Keep in mind the three activities and their order—feeding time, waketime, then naptime. Review Chapter 7, *Establishing Your Baby's Routine*, to determine how many feedings are appropriate in a 24-hour period given your child's age. For example, if your baby is three months old, he should be on four to five feedings a day. If he is six months old, he should be on three meals a day with a nursing period or a bottle just before bed.

    If you were in the habit of rocking or nursing your baby to sleep at naptime, now is the time to eliminate that practice.

2. Review Chapter 9, *When Your Baby Cries*, and be prepared for some crying. You are moving from a high-comfort style of sleep manipulation to basic training in sleep skills. Initially, your baby will not like this needed change, but it is necessary.

    In moments of parental stress, be comforted in knowing that your baby will not feel abandoned since you have decided that the best thing for him is learning how to fall asleep on his own. Continue to think about and look toward the long-term benefits. Your proactive response is best for the baby and the entire family.

3. Do not feel the necessity to check your baby every 5 minutes while he is crying. If you go into his room, try to do so without him seeing you. If necessary, move the crib so you can see the baby, but he cannot see you. If you feel you must soothe him, go in briefly and pat him on the back. With a soft voice tell him, "It's all

right," then quietly leave. As a result, your baby will do one of two things: be comforted and fall asleep, or roar even louder.

If he chooses the latter, do not be discouraged. His crying only means that he has not developed the ability to settle himself. That goal is exactly what you are working toward.

4. Be patient and consistent. For some parents, success comes after one night; for others, it comes after two weeks. The norm, however, is three to five days.

SUMMARY

Retraining is always more difficult than training correctly from the start, but it needs to be done. Parents who love their babies give them what they need. Young children need a good night's sleep.

Moms who have made the transition from sleepless nights to peaceful sleep report that their children not only gain the advantage of continuous nighttime sleep, but their daytime disposition also changes. They appear happier, more content, and definitely more manageable. We trust this result will be the case with your baby.

Many blessings on your family.

Gary Ezzo and Dr. Robert Bucknam

NEXT STOP:
BABYWISE II
(Parenting Your Pretoddler, 5-15 Months)

Throughout the process of your baby's growth there are both constant and variable factors influencing development. As your child approaches the pretoddler phase, the variables of growth begin to play a more dominant role. How will you respond to those variables? Certainly not by abandoning that which has brought you so much success—your baby's routine. You rightly respond to the emerging variables by knowing what to expect of your pretoddler, when to expect it, and at what ages different patterns of behavior will normally emerge into mature forms. Knowing the progressive nature of growth enables a parent to set standards of expected behavior and provide the guidance needed to reach behavior goals.

What behavior can be expected from your pretoddler? Of what is he capable? *BABYWISE II* will emphasize the importance of learning patterns. Those patterns form learning structures that assist the child throughout his early development. As cartilage strengthens and turns into bone, so also learning patterns develop and form the infrastructure for future moral and academic learning. The first patterns established should be the right patterns. *BABYWISE II* is fun, informative, and most important, extremely practical.

For more information, write: *Growing Families International*, 9259 Eton Ave., Chatsworth, CA 91311.

ENDNOTES

Chapter 1

1. The term "democratic parenting" was popularized in the mid-1940s by educational theorists Arnold Gesell and Rudolf Dreikurs.

2. The theory of democratic parenting is based on two assumptions: that a child has no natural propensity for wayward behavior, and that parental authority creates conflict. Therefore, the theory purports that by eliminating or minimizing parental authority, parents can seriously reduce conflict in their child's life. This theory is overly optimistic.

Chapter 2

3. Dr. Rupert Rogers wrote on the problems of breast-feeding during the 1930s and 1940s. He told mothers to be old-fashioned. What did he mean by that? He said go back to nursing periods arranged as follows: 6:00 a.m., 9:00 a.m., noon, 3:00 p.m., 6:00 p.m., and 10:00 p.m., and once when the baby woke in the night. Although that type of feeding was still a schedule, it was not referred to as such. The term "schedule" referred to a nursing technique more than a routine. *Mother's Encyclopedia* (New York: The Parents Institute Inc., 1951), p. 122.

4. We do not take issue with a mother who chooses to breast-feed longer than a year because she enjoys that special time. We take issue with the suggestion that the child has a psychological need inherent at birth and if not allowed access to his mother's breast, his future emotional health is put at risk.

Chapter 4

5. This conclusion was drawn from a study based on thirty-two mother-infant pairs observed over two years. Sixteen families were from the La Leche League, and the other sixteen were not. "Sleep-Wake Patterns of Breast-Fed Infants in the First Two Years of Life," *Pediatrics,* Vol. 77, No. 3, March 1986, p. 328.

6. Even as we write this edition, a two-month-old girl was smothered to death by her sleeping parent. (See "Baby dies after being hurt by dad accidentally," Orange County Register, February 23, 1994.)

Chapter 5

7. A baby's immune system is developed by two sources. During pregnancy, disease-fighting proteins called antibodies pass from the mother's blood to the baby's blood. They provide temporary protection against the many illnesses to which the mother has been exposed. After birth, the baby's immune system is enhanced with breast milk. That is done two ways: (1) By the passing of the mother's antibodies through the milk, which are then absorbed into the child's bloodstream. (2) By way of the bifidus factor. Infants are born with millions of tiny organisms in a semidormant state, which are members of the *Lactobacillus-bifidus* family. Their growth is stimulated by certain elements in the mother's milk. As these organisms grow, they produce acetic and lactic acids that prevent the growth of many disease-producing organisms, such as E. coli and dysentery bacilli. This does not mean that bottle-fed babies have no immune system; they do, but it is not as protective.

8. Breast-feeding mothers are sometimes warned not to use a bottle. The concern is over "nipple confusion." The belief is that a baby will become confused and refuse the breast if offered a bottle. Although under normal circumstances there will be no need to introduce a bottle to the breast-fed infant in the first month, there will come a time when the bottle will be a welcome friend. The bottle allows other family members to share in the joy of feeding the newest family member. Though babies do not become confused over nipples, they may demonstrate a preference for one over another. You can guide their choice.

Chapter 9

9. Crying periods vary with each child. When you include their late afternoon fussy time, a normal baby may cry as much as 3 hours total per day, with 5-45 minutes in any one session.

Chapter 10

10. Michael E. Lamb, Ph.D., from the Department of Pediatrics at the University of Utah Medical School, summarizes our position: "The preponderance of the evidence thus suggests that extended contact [the bonding theory] has no clear effects on maternal behavior" *Pediatrics*, Vol. 70, No. 5, November 1982, p. 768.